Complete Works: Four

This book is Volume Four of the Collected Works of Harold Pinter.

WORKS BY HAROLD PINTER
PUBLISHED BY GROVE PRESS

Betrayal

The Birthday Party *and* The Room

The Caretaker *and* The Dumb Waiter

COMPLETE WORKS: ONE (The Birthday Party; The Room; The Dumb Waiter; A Slight Ache; A Night Out; The Black and White; The Examination)

COMPLETE WORKS: TWO (The Caretaker; The Dwarfs; The Collection; The Lover; Night School; Revue Sketches [Trouble in the Works; The Black and White; Request Stop; Last to Go; Special Offer])

COMPLETE WORKS: THREE (The Homecoming; Landscape; Silence; The Basement; Revue Sketches [Night; That's All; That's Your Trouble; Interview; Applicant; Dialogue for Three]; Tea Party [Play]; Tea Party [Short Story]; Mac)

FIVE SCREENPLAYS (The Servant; The Pumkin Eater; The Berlin Memorandum [The Quiller Memorandum]; Accident; The Go-Between)

The Homecoming

Landscape *and* Silence

No Man's Land

Old Times

One for the Road

100 Poems by 100 Poets (*selected by Harold Pinter, Geoffrey Godbert, and Anthony Astbury*)

Other Places: Three Plays

Poems and Prose: 1949–1977

The Proust Screenplay

THREE PLAYS (The Collection; A Slight Ache; The Dwarfs)

HAROLD PINTER

Complete Works: Four

Old Times
No Man's Land
Betrayal
Monologue
Family Voices

With an introduction by the author

GROVE PRESS
NEW YORK

First published in Great Britain in 1981
by Eyre Methuen Ltd, 11 New Fetter Lane,
London ECP4P 4EE, England.

Published by Grove Press
a division of Wheatland Corporation
920 Broadway
New York, N.Y. 10010

First Black Cat Edition 1981
ISBN:0-8021-5050-0
Library of Congress Catalog Card Number: 81-47696

Manufactured in Great Britain

10 9 8 7 6 5 4 3 2

Contents

Chronology   *page* vii

Introduction   ix

OLD TIMES   I

NO MAN'S LAND   73

BETRAYAL   155

MONOLOGUE   269

FAMILY VOICES   279

Harold Pinter: A Chronology

Year of writing		*First performance*
1954–5	The Black and White	(short story)
1955	The Examination	(short story)
1957	The Room	15 May 1957
1957	The Birthday Party	28 April 1958
1957	The Dumb Waiter	21 January 1960
1958	A Slight Ache	29 July 1959
1958	The Hothouse	24 April 1980
1959	Revue sketches—	
	Trouble in the Works; The Black and White	15 July 1959
	Request Stop; Last to Go; Special Offer	23 September 1959
	That's Your Trouble; That's All; Applicant; Interview; Dialogue for Three	February–March 1964
1959	A Night Out	1 March 1960
1959	The Caretaker	27 April 1960
1960	Night School	21 July 1960
1960	The Dwarfs	2 December 1960
1961	The Collection	11 May 1961
1962	The Lover	28 March 1963
1963	Tea Party	(short story)
1964	Tea Party	25 March 1965
1964	The Homecoming	3 June 1965
1966	The Basement	28 February 1967
1967	Landscape	25 April 1968
1968	Silence	2 July 1969
1969	Night	9 April 1969
1970	Old Times	1 June 1971
1972	Monologue	10 April 1973
1974	No Man's Land	23 April 1975
1978	Betrayal	15 November 1978
1980	Family Voices	22 January 1981
1982	Victoria Station	performed with *Family Voices* as a trilogy entitled *Other Places* in 1982
	A Kind of Alaska	
1984	One for the Road	15 March 1984

Introduction

A speech made by Harold Pinter in Hamburg, West Germany, on being awarded the 1970 German Shakespeare Prize.

When I was informed that I was to be given this award my reaction was to be startled, even bewildered, while at the same time to feel deeply gratified by this honour. I remain honoured and slightly bewildered, but also frightened. What frightens me is that I have been asked to speak to you today. If I find writing difficult I find giving a public address doubly so.

Once, many years ago, I found myself engaged uneasily in a public discussion on the theatre. Someone asked me what my work was 'about.' I replied with no thought at all and merely to frustrate this line of enquiry: 'The weasel under the cocktail cabinet.' That was a great mistake. Over the years I have seen that remark quoted in a number of learned columns. It has now seemingly acquired a profound significance, and is seen to be a highly relevant and meaningful observation about my own work. But for me the remark meant precisely nothing. Such are the dangers of speaking in public.

In what way can one talk about one's work? I'm a writer, not a critic. When I use the word work I mean work. I regard myself as nothing more than a working man.

I am moved by the fact that the selection committee for the Shakespeare Prize has judged my work, in the context of this award, as worthy of it, but it's impossible for me to understand the reasons that led them to their decision. I'm at the other end of the telescope. The language used, the opinions given, the approvals and objections engendered by one's work happen in a sense outside one's actual experience of it, since the core of that experience consists in writing the stuff. I have a particular relationship with the words I put down on paper and the characters which emerge from them which no-one else can share with me. And perhaps that's why I remain bewildered by praise and really quite indifferent to insult. Praise and insult refer to someone called Pinter. I don't know the man they're talking about. I know the plays, but in a totally different way, in a quite private way.

If I am to talk at all I prefer to talk practically about practical matters, but that's no more than a pious hope, since one invariably slips into theorising, almost without noticing it. And I distrust theory. In whatever capacity I have worked in the theatre, and apart from writing, I have done quite a bit of acting and a certain amount of directing for the stage, I have found that theory, as such, has never been helpful; either to myself, or, I have noticed, to few of my colleagues. The best sort of collaborative working relationship in the theatre, in my view, consists in a kind of stumbling erratic shorthand, through which facts are lost, collided with, fumbled, found again. One excellent director I know has never been known to complete a sentence. He has such instinctive surety and almost subliminal powers of communication that the actors respond to his words before he has said them.

I don't want to imply that I am counselling lack of intelligence as a working aid. On the contrary, I am referring to an intelligence brought to bear on practical and relevant matters, on matters which are active and alive and specific, an intelligence working with others to find the legitimate and therefore compulsory facts and make them concrete for us on the stage. A rehearsal period which consists of philosophical discourse or political treatise does not get the curtain up at eight o'clock.

I have referred to facts, by which I mean theatrical facts. It is true to say that theatrical facts do not easily disclose their secrets, and it is very easy, when they prove stubborn, to distort them, to make them into something else, or to pretend they never existed. This happens more often in the theatre than we care to recognize and is proof either of incompetence or fundamental contempt for the work in hand.

I believe myself that when a writer looks at the blank of the word he has not yet written, or when actors and directors arrive at a given moment on stage, there is only one proper thing that can take place at that moment, and that that thing, that gesture, that word on the page, must alone be found, and once found, scrupulously protected. I think I am talking about necessary shape, both as regards a play and its production.

If there is, as I believe, a necessary, an obligatory shape which a play demands of its writer, then I have never been able to achieve it myself. I have always finished the last draft of a play with a mixture of feelings: relief, disbelief, exhilaration, and a certainty that if I could only wring the play's neck once more it might yield once more to me, that I could get it better, that I could get the better of it, perhaps. But that's impossible. You create the word and in a certain way the word, in finding its own life, stares you out, is obdurate, and more often than not defeats you. You create the characters and they prove to be very tough. They observe you, their writer, warily. It may sound absurd, but I believe I am speaking the truth when I say that I have suffered two kinds of pain through my characters. I have witnessed *their* pain when I am in the act of distorting them, of falsifying them, and I have witnessed their contempt. I have suffered pain when I have been unable to get to the quick of them, when they wilfully elude me, when they withdraw into the shadows. And there's a third and rarer pain. That is when the right word, or the right act jolts them or stills them into their proper life. When that happens the pain is worth having. When that happens I am ready to take them into the nearest bar and buy drinks all round. And I hope they would forgive me my trespasses against them and do the same for me. But there is no question that quite a conflict takes place between the writer and his characters and on the whole I would say the characters are the winners. And that's as it should be, I think. Where a writer sets out a blueprint for his characters, and keeps them rigidly to it, where they do not at any time upset his applecart, where he has mastered them, he has also killed them, or rather terminated their birth, and he has a dead play on his hands.

Sometimes, the director says to me in rehearsal: 'Why does she say this?' I reply: 'Wait a minute, let me look at the text.' I do so, and perhaps I say: 'Doesn't she say this because he said *that*, two pages ago?' Or I say: 'Because that's what she feels.' Or: 'Because she feels something else, and therefore says that.' Or: 'I haven't the faintest idea. But somehow we have to find out.' Sometimes I learn quite a lot from rehearsals.

I have been very fortunate, in my life, in the people I've worked with, and my association with Peter Hall and the Royal Shakespeare Company has, particularly, been greatly satisfying. Peter Hall and I, working together, have found that the image must be pursued with the greatest vigilance, calmly, and once found, must be sharpened, graded, accurately focused and maintained, and that the key word is economy, economy of movement and gesture, of emotion and its expression, both the internal and the external in specific and exact relation to each other, so that there is no wastage and no mess. These are hardly revolutionary conclusions, but I hope no less worthy of restatement for that.

I may appear to be laying too heavy an emphasis on method and technique as opposed to content, but this is not in fact the case. I am not suggesting that the disciplines to which I have been referring be imposed upon the action in terms of a device, or as a formal convenience. What is made evident before us on the stage can clearly only be made fully evident where the content of the scene has been defined. But I do not understand this definition as one arrived at through the intellect, but a definition made by the actors, using quite a different system. In other words, if I now bring various criteria to bear upon a production, these are not intellectual concepts but facts forged through experience of active participation with good actors and, I hope, a living text.

What am I writing about? Not the weasel under the cocktail cabinet.

I am not concerned with making general statements. I am not interested in theatre used simply as a means of self-expression on the part of the people engaged in it. I find in so much group theatre, under the sweat and assault and noise, nothing but valueless generalizations, naive and quite un-fruitful.

I can sum up none of my plays. I can describe none of them, except to say: That is what happened. That is what they said. That is what they did.

I am aware, sometimes, of an insistence in my mind. Images, characters, insisting upon being written. You can pour a drink, make a telephone call or run round the park, and sometimes succeed in suffocating them. You know they're going to make your life hell. But at other times they're un-avoidable and you're compelled to try to do them some kind of justice. And while it may be hell, it's certainly for me the best kind of hell to be in.

However, I find it ironic that I have come here to receive this distinguished award as a writer, and that at the moment I am writing nothing and can write nothing. I don't know why. It's a very bad feeling, I know that, but I must say I want more than anything else to fill up a blank page again, and to feel that strange thing happen, birth through fingertips. When you can't write you feel you've been banished from yourself.

Old Times

Old Times was first presented by the Royal Shakespeare Company at the Aldwych Theatre, London, on 1st June, 1971, with the following cast:

DEELEY	Colin Blakely
KATE	Dorothy Tutin
ANNA	Vivien Merchant

All in their early forties

Directed by Peter Hall

A converted farmhouse

A long window up centre. Bedroom door up left. Front door up right.

Spare modern furniture. Two sofas. An armchair.

Autumn. Night.

ACT ONE

Light dim. Three figures discerned.

DEELEY *slumped in armchair, still.*
KATE *curled on a sofa, still.*
ANNA *standing at the window, looking out.*

Silence

Lights up on DEELEY *and* KATE, *smoking cigarettes.*

ANNA's *figure remains still in dim light at the window.*

KATE

(*Reflectively.*) Dark.

Pause

DEELEY

Fat or thin?

KATE

Fuller than me. I think.

Pause

DEELEY

She was then?

KATE

I think so.

DEELEY

She may not be now.

Pause

Was she your best friend?

KATE

Oh, what does that mean?

DEELEY

What?

KATE

The word friend . . . when you look back . . . all that time.

DEELEY

Can't you remember what you felt?

Pause

KATE

It is a very long time.

DEELEY

But you remember her. She remembers you. Or why would she be coming here tonight?

KATE

I suppose because she remembers me.

Pause

DEELEY

Did you *think* of her as your best friend?

KATE

She was my only friend.

DEELEY

Your best and only.

KATE

My one and only.

Pause

If you have only one of something you can't say it's the best of anything.

DEELEY

Because you have nothing to compare it with?

KATE

Mmnn.

Pause

DEELEY

(*Smiling.*) She was incomparable.

KATE

Oh, I'm sure she wasn't.

Pause

DEELEY

I didn't know you had so few friends.

KATE

I had none. None at all. Except her.

DEELEY

Why her?

KATE

I don't know.

Pause

She was a thief. She used to steal things.

DEELEY

Who from?

KATE

Me.

DEELEY

What things?

KATE

Bits and pieces. Underwear.

DEELEY *chuckles*.

DEELEY

Will you remind her?

KATE

Oh . . . I don't think so.

Pause

DEELEY

Is that what attracted you to her?

KATE

What?

DEELEY

The fact that she was a thief.

KATE

No.

Pause

DEELEY

Are you looking forward to seeing her?

KATE

No.

DEELEY

I am. I shall be very interested.

KATE

In what?

DEELEY

In you. I'll be watching you.

KATE

Me? Why?

DEELEY

To see if she's the same person.

KATE

You think you'll find that out through me?

DEELEY

Definitely.

Pause

KATE

I hardly remember her. I've almost totally forgotten her.

Pause

DEELEY

Any idea what she drinks?

KATE

None.

DEELEY

She may be a vegetarian.

KATE

Ask her.

DEELEY

It's too late. You've cooked your casserole.

Pause

Why isn't she married? I mean, why isn't she bringing her husband?

KATE

Ask her.

DEELEY

Do I have to ask her everything?

KATE

Do you want me to ask your questions for you?

DEELEY

No. Not at all.

Pause

KATE

Of course she's married.

DEELEY

How do you know?

KATE

Everyone's married.

DEELEY

Then why isn't she bringing her husband?

KATE

Isn't she?

Pause

DEELEY

Did she mention a husband in her letter?

KATE

No.

DEELEY

What do you think he'd be like? I mean, what sort of man would she have married? After all, she was your best – your only – friend. You must have some idea. What kind of man would he be?

KATE

I have no idea.

DEELEY

Haven't you any curiosity?

KATE

You forget. I know her.

DEELEY

You haven't seen her for twenty years.

KATE

You've never seen her. There's a difference.

Pause

DEELEY

At least the casserole is big enough for four.

KATE

You said she was a vegetarian.

Pause

DEELEY

Did *she* have many friends?

KATE

Oh . . . the normal amount, I suppose.

DEELEY

Normal? What's normal? You had none.

KATE

One.

DEELEY

Is that normal?

Pause

She . . . had quite a lot of friends, did she?

KATE

Hundreds.

DEELEY

You met them?

KATE

Not all, I think. But after all, we were living together. There were visitors, from time to time. I met them.

DEELEY

Her visitors?

KATE

What?

DEELEY

Her visitors. Her friends. You had no friends.

KATE

Her friends, yes.

DEELEY

You met them.

Pause

(*Abruptly.*) You lived together?

KATE

Mmmnn?

DEELEY

You lived together?

KATE

Of course.

DEELEY

I didn't know that.

KATE

Didn't you?

DEELEY

You never told me that. I thought you just knew each other.

KATE

We did.

DEELEY

But in fact you lived with each other.

KATE

Of course we did. How else would she steal my underwear from me? In the street?

Pause

DEELEY

I knew you had shared with someone at one time . . .

Pause

But I didn't know it was her.

KATE

Of course it was.

Pause

DEELEY

Anyway, none of this matters.

ANNA *turns from the window, speaking, and moves down to them, eventually sitting on the second sofa.*

ANNA

Queuing all night, the rain, do you remember? my goodness, the Albert Hall, Covent Garden, what did we eat? to look back, half the night, to do things we loved, we were young then of course, but what stamina, and to work in the morning, and to a concert, or the opera, or the ballet, that night, you haven't forgotten? and then riding on top of the bus down Kensington High Street, and the bus conductors, and then dashing for the matches for the gasfire and then I suppose scrambled eggs, or did we? who cooked? both giggling and chattering, both huddling to the heat, then bed and sleeping, and all the hustle and bustle in the morning, rushing for the bus again for work, lunchtimes in Green Park, exchanging all our news, with our very own sandwiches, innocent girls, innocent secretaries, and then the night to come, and goodness knows what excitement in store, I mean the sheer expectation of it all, the looking-for-wardness of it all, and so poor, but to be poor and young, and a girl, in London then . . . and the cafés we found, almost private ones, weren't they? where artists and writers and sometimes actors collected, and others with dancers, we sat hardly breath-ing with our coffee, heads bent, so as not to be seen, so as not to disturb, so as not to distract, and listened and listened to all those words, all those cafés and all those people, creative un-doubtedly, and does it still exist I wonder? do you know? can you tell me?

Slight pause

DEELEY

We rarely get to London.

KATE *stands, goes to a small table and pours coffee from a pot.*

KATE

Yes, I remember.

She adds milk and sugar to one cup and takes it to ANNA. *She takes a black coffee to* DEELEY *and then sits with her own.*

DEELEY

(*to* ANNA.) Do you drink brandy?

ANNA

I would love some brandy.

DEELEY *pours brandy for all and hands the glasses. He remains standing with his own.*

ANNA

Listen. What silence. Is it always as silent?

DEELEY

It's quite silent here, yes. Normally.

Pause

You can hear the sea sometimes if you listen very carefully.

ANNA

How wise you were to choose this part of the world, and how sensible and courageous of you both to stay permanently in such a silence.

DEELEY

My work takes me away quite often, of course. But Kate stays here.

ANNA

No one who lived here would want to go far. I would not want to go far, I would be afraid of going far, lest when I returned the house would be gone.

DEELEY

Lest?

ANNA

What?

DEELEY

The word lest. Haven't heard it for a long time.

Pause

KATE

Sometimes I walk to the sea. There aren't many people. It's a long beach.

Pause

ANNA

But I would miss London, nevertheless. But of course I was a girl in London. We were girls together.

DEELEY

I wish I had known you both then.

ANNA

Do you?

DEELEY

Yes.

DEELEY *pours more brandy for himself.*

ANNA

You have a wonderful casserole.

DEELEY

What?

ANNA

I mean wife. So sorry. A wonderful wife.

DEELEY

Ah.

ANNA

I was referring to the casserole. I was referring to your wife's cooking.

DEELEY

You're not a vegetarian, then?

ANNA

No. Oh no.

DEELEY

Yes, you need good food in the country, substantial food, to keep you going, all the air . . . you know.

Pause

KATE

Yes, I quite like those kind of things, doing it.

ANNA

What kind of things?

KATE

Oh, you know, that sort of thing.

Pause

DEELEY

Do you mean cooking?

KATE

All that thing.

ANNA

We weren't terribly elaborate in cooking, didn't have the time, but every so often dished up an incredibly enormous stew, guzzled the lot, and then more often than not sat up half the night reading Yeats.

Pause

(*To herself.*) Yes. Every so often. More often than not.

ANNA *stands, walks to the window.*

And the sky is so still.

Pause

Can you see that tiny ribbon of light? Is that the sea? Is that the horizon?

DEELEY

You live on a very different coast.

ANNA

Oh, very different. I live on a volcanic island.

DEELEY

I know it.

ANNA

Oh, do you?

DEELEY

I've been there.

Pause

ANNA

I'm so delighted to be here.

DEELEY

It's nice I know for Katey to see you. She hasn't many friends.

ANNA

She has you.

DEELEY

She hasn't made many friends, although there's been every opportunity for her to do so.

ANNA

Perhaps she has all she wants.

DEELEY

She lacks curiosity.

ANNA

Perhaps she's happy.

Pause

KATE

Are you talking about me?

DEELEY

Yes.

ANNA

She was always a dreamer.

DEELEY

She likes taking long walks. All that. You know. Raincoat on.
Off down the lane, hands deep in pockets. All that kind of
thing.

ANNA *turns to look at* KATE.

ANNA

Yes.

DEELEY

Sometimes I take her face in my hands and look at it.

ANNA

Really?

DEELEY

Yes, I look at it, holding it in my hands. Then I kind of let it
go, take my hands away, leave it floating.

KATE

My head is quite fixed. I have it on.

DEELEY

(*To* ANNA.) It just floats away.

ANNA

She was always a dreamer.

ANNA *sits.*

Sometimes, walking, in the park, I'd say to her, you're dreaming, you're dreaming, wake up, what are you dreaming? and

she'd look round at me, flicking her hair, and look at me as if I were part of her dream.

Pause

One day she said to me, I've slept through Friday. No you haven't, I said, what do you mean? I've slept right through Friday, she said. But today is Friday, I said, it's been Friday all day, it's now Friday night, you haven't slept through Friday. Yes I have, she said, I've slept right through it, today is Saturday.

DEELEY

You mean she literally didn't know what day it was?

ANNA

No.

KATE

Yes I did. It was Saturday.

Pause

DEELEY

What month are we in?

KATE

September.

Pause

DEELEY

We're forcing her to think. We must see you more often. You're a healthy influence.

ANNA

But she was always a charming companion.

DEELEY

Fun to live with?

ANNA

Delightful.

DEELEY

Lovely to look at, delightful to know.

ANNA

Ah, those songs. We used to play them, all of them, all the time, late at night, lying on the floor, lovely old things. Sometimes I'd look at her face, but she was quite unaware of my gaze.

DEELEY

Gaze?

ANNA

What?

DEELEY

The word gaze. Don't hear it very often.

ANNA

Yes, quite unaware of it. She was totally absorbed.

DEELEY

In Lovely to look at, delightful to know?

KATE

(*To* ANNA.) I don't know that song. Did we have it?

DEELEY

(*Singing, to* KATE.) You're lovely to look at, delightful to know . . .

ANNA

Oh we did. Yes, of course. We had them all.

DEELEY

(*Singing.*) Blue moon, I see you standing alone . . .

ANNA

(*Singing.*) The way you comb your hair . . .

DEELEY

(*Singing.*) Oh no they can't take that away from me . . .

ANNA

(*Singing.*) Oh but you're lovely, with your smile so warm . . .

DEELEY

(*Singing.*) I've got a woman crazy for me. She's funny that way.

Slight pause

ANNA

(*Singing.*) You are the promised kiss of springtime . . .

DEELEY

(*Singing.*) And someday I'll know that moment divine,
         When all the things you are, are mine!

Slight pause

ANNA

(*Singing.*) I get no kick from champagne,
Mere alcohol doesn't thrill me at all,
So tell me why should it be true –

DEELEY

(*Singing.*) That I get a kick out of you?

Pause

ANNA

(*Singing.*) They asked me how I knew
My true love was true,
I of course replied,
Something here inside
Cannot be denied.

DEELEY

(*Singing.*) When a lovely flame dies . . .

ANNA

(*Singing.*) Smoke gets in your eyes.

Pause

DEELEY

(*Singing.*) The sigh of midnight trains in empty stations . . .

Pause

ANNA

(*Singing.*) The park at evening when the bell has sounded . . .

Pause

DEELEY

(*Singing.*) The smile of Garbo and the scent of roses . . .

ANNA

(*Singing.*) The waiters whistling as the last bar closes . . .

DEELEY

(*Singing.*) Oh, how the ghost of you clings . . .

Pause

They don't make them like that any more.

Silence

What happened to me was this. I popped into a fleapit to see Odd Man Out. Some bloody awful summer afternoon, walking in no direction. I remember thinking there was something familiar about the neighbourhood and suddenly recalled that it was in this very neighbourhood that my father bought me my first tricycle, the only tricycle in fact I ever possessed. Anyway, there was the bicycle shop and there was this fleapit showing Odd Man Out and there were two usherettes standing in the foyer and one of them was stroking her breasts and the other one was saying 'dirty bitch' and the one stroking her breasts was saying 'mmnnn' with a very sensual relish and smiling at her fellow usherette, so I marched in on this excruciatingly hot summer afternoon in the middle of nowhere and watched Odd Man Out and thought Robert Newton was fantastic. And I still think he was fantastic. And I would commit murder for him, even now. And there was only one other person in the cinema, one other person in the whole of the whole cinema, and there she is. And there she was, very dim, very still, placed more or less I would say at the dead centre of the auditorium. I was off centre and have remained so. And I left when the film was over, noticing, even though James Mason was dead, that the first usherette appeared to be utterly exhausted, and I stood for a moment in the sun, thinking I suppose about something and then this girl came out and I think looked about her and I said wasn't Robert Newton fantastic, and she said something or other, Christ knows what, but looked at me, and I thought Jesus this is it, I've made a catch, this is a trueblue pickup, and when we had sat down in the café with tea she looked into her cup and then up at me and told me she thought Robert Newton was remarkable. So it was Robert Newton who brought us together and it is only Robert Newton who can tear us apart.

Pause

ANNA

F. J. McCormick was good too.

DEELEY

I know F. J. McCormick was good too. But he didn't bring us together.

Pause

DEELEY

You've seen the film then?

ANNA

Yes.

DEELEY

When?

ANNA

Oh . . . long ago.

Pause

DEELEY

(*To* KATE.) Remember that film?

KATE

Oh yes. Very well.

Pause

DEELEY

I think I am right in saying the next time we met we held hands. I held her cool hand, as she walked by me, and I said something which made her smile, and she looked at me, didn't you, flicking her hair back, and I thought she was even more fantastic than Robert Newton.

Pause

And then at a slightly later stage our naked bodies met, hers cool, warm, highly agreeable, and I wondered what Robert Newton would think of this. What would he think of this I wondered as I touched her profoundly all over.
(*To* ANNA.) What do you think he'd think?

ANNA

I never met Robert Newton but I do know I know what you mean. There are some things one remembers even though they may never have happened. There are things I remember which may never have happened but as I recall them so they take place.

DEELEY

What?

ANNA

This man crying in our room. One night late I returned and found him sobbing, his hand over his face, sitting in the armchair, all crumpled in the armchair and Katey sitting on the bed with a mug of coffee and no one spoke to me, no one spoke, no one looked up. There was nothing I could do. I undressed and switched out the light and got into my bed, the curtains were thin, the light from the street came in, Katey still, on her bed, the man sobbed, the light came in, it flicked the wall, there was a slight breeze, the curtains occasionally shook, there was nothing but sobbing, suddenly it stopped. The man came over to me, quickly, looked down at me, but I would have absolutely nothing to do with him, nothing.

Pause

No, no, I'm quite wrong . . . he didn't move quickly . . . that's quite wrong . . . he moved . . . very slowly, the light was bad, and stopped. He stood in the centre of the room. He looked at us both, at our beds. Then he turned towards me. He approached my bed. He bent down over me. But I would have nothing to do with him, absolutely nothing.

Pause

DEELEY

What kind of man was he?

ANNA

But after a while I heard him go out. I heard the front door close, and footsteps in the street, then silence, then the footsteps fade away, and then silence.

Pause

But then sometime later in the night I woke up and looked across the room to her bed and saw two shapes.

DEELEY

He'd come back!

ANNA

He was lying across her lap on her bed.

DEELEY

A man in the dark across my wife's lap?

Pause

ANNA

But then in the early morning . . . he had gone.

DEELEY

Thank Christ for that.

ANNA

It was as if he had never been.

DEELEY

Of course he'd been. He went twice and came once.

Pause

Well, what an exciting story that was.

Pause

What did he look like, this fellow?

ANNA

Oh, I never saw his face clearly. I don't know.

DEELEY

But was he – ?

KATE *stands. She goes to a small table, takes a cigarette from a box and lights it. She looks down at* ANNA.

KATE

You talk of me as if I were dead.

ANNA

No, no, you weren't dead, you were so lively, so animated, you used to laugh –

DEELEY

Of course you did. I made you smile myself, didn't I? walking along the street, holding hands. You smiled fit to bust.

ANNA

Yes, she could be so ... animated.

DEELEY

Animated is no word for it. When she smiled ... how can I describe it?

ANNA

Her eyes lit up.

DEELEY

I couldn't have put it better myself.

DEELEY *stands, goes to cigarette box, picks it up, smiles at* KATE.
KATE *looks at him, watches him light a cigarette, takes the box
from him, crosses to* ANNA, *offers her a cigarette.* ANNA *takes one.*

ANNA

You weren't dead. Ever. In any way.

KATE

I said you talk about me as if I *am* dead. Now.

ANNA

How can you say that? How can you say that, when I'm looking
at you now, seeing you so shyly poised over me, looking down
at me –

DEELEY

Stop that!

Pause

KATE *sits.*
DEELEY *pours a drink.*

DEELEY

Myself I was a student then, juggling with my future, wondering should I bejasus saddle myself with a slip of a girl not long
out of her swaddling clothes whose only claim to virtue was
silence but who lacked any sense of fixedness, any sense of
decisiveness, but was compliant only to the shifting winds,
with which she went, but not *the* winds, and certainly not my
winds, such as they are, but I suppose winds that only she

understood, and that of course with no understanding whatsoever, at least as I understand the word, at least that's the way I
figured it. A classic female figure, I said to myself, or is it a
classic female posture, one way or the other long outworn.

Pause

That's the position as I saw it then. I mean, that is my categorical pronouncement on the position as I saw it then. Twenty
years ago.

Silence

ANNA

When I heard that Katey was married my heart leapt with joy.

DEELEY

How did the news reach you?

ANNA

From a friend.

Pause

Yes, it leapt with joy. Because you see I knew she never did
things loosely or carelessly, recklessly. Some people throw a
stone into a river to see if the water's too cold for jumping,
others, a few others, will always wait for the ripples before they
will jump.

DEELEY

Some people do *what*? (*To* KATE.) What did she say?

ANNA

And I knew that Katey would always wait not just for the first
emergence of ripple but for the ripples to pervade and pervade

the surface, for of course as you know ripples on the surface indicate a shimmering in depth down through every particle of water down to the river bed, but even when she felt that happen, when she was assured it was happening, she still might not jump. But in this case she did jump and I knew therefore she had fallen in love truly and was glad. And I deduced it must also have happened to you.

DEELEY

You mean the ripples?

ANNA

If you like.

DEELEY

Do men ripple too?

ANNA

Some, I would say.

DEELEY

I see.

Pause

ANNA

And later when I found out the kind of man you were I was doubly delighted because I knew Katey had always been interested in the arts.

KATE

I was interested once in the arts, but I can't remember now which ones they were.

ANNA

Don't tell me you've forgotten our days at the Tate? and how we explored London and all the old churches and all the old buildings, I mean those that were left from the bombing, in the City and south of the river in Lambeth and Greenwich? Oh my goodness. Oh yes. And the Sunday papers! I could never get her away from the review pages. She ravished them, and then insisted we visit that gallery, or this theatre, or that chamber concert, but of course there was so much, so much to see and to hear, in lovely London then, that sometimes we missed things, or had no more money, and so missed some things. For example, I remember one Sunday she said to me, looking up from the paper, come quick, quick, come with me quickly, and we seized our handbags and went, on a bus, to some totally obscure, some totally unfamiliar district and, almost alone, saw a wonderful film called Odd Man Out.

Silence

DEELEY

Yes, I do quite a bit of travelling in my job.

ANNA

Do you enjoy it?

DEELEY

Enormously. Enormously.

ANNA

Do you go far?

DEELEY

I travel the globe in my job.

ANNA

And poor Katey when you're away? What does she do?

ANNA *looks at* KATE.

KATE

Oh, I continue.

ANNA

Is he away for long periods?

KATE

I think, sometimes. Are you?

ANNA

You leave your wife for such long periods? How can you?

DEELEY

I have to do a lot of travelling in my job.

ANNA

(*To* KATE.) I think I must come and keep you company when he's away.

DEELEY

Won't your husband miss you?

ANNA

Of course. But he would understand.

DEELEY

Does he understand now?

ANNA

Of course.

DEELEY

We had a vegetarian dish prepared for him.

ANNA

He's not a vegetarian. In fact he's something of a gourmet. We live in a rather fine villa and have done so for many years. It's very high up, on the cliffs.

DEELEY

You eat well up there, eh?

ANNA

I would say so, yes.

DEELEY

Yes, I know Sicily slightly. Just slightly. Taormina. Do you live in Taormina?

ANNA

Just outside.

DEELEY

Just outside, yes. Very high up. Yes, I've probably caught a glimpse of your villa.

Pause

My work took me to Sicily. My work concerns itself with life all over, you see, in every part of the globe. With people all over the globe. I use the word globe because the word world possesses emotional political sociological and psychological pretensions and resonances which I prefer as a matter of choice to do without, or shall I say to steer clear of, or if you like to reject. How's the yacht?

ANNA

Oh, very well.

DEELEY

Captain steer a straight course?

ANNA

As straight as we wish, when we wish it.

DEELEY

Don't you find England damp, returning?

ANNA

Rather beguilingly so.

DEELEY

Rather beguilingly so? (*To himself.*) What the hell does she mean by that?

Pause

Well, any time your husband finds himself in this direction my little wife will be only too glad to put the old pot on the old gas stove and dish him up something luscious if not voluptuous. No trouble.

Pause

I suppose his business interests kept him from making the trip. What's his name? Gian Carlo or Per Paulo?

KATE

(*To* ANNA.) Do you have marble floors?

ANNA

Yes.

KATE

Do you walk in bare feet on them?

ANNA

Yes. But I wear sandals on the terrace, because it can be rather severe on the soles.

KATE

The sun, you mean? The heat.

ANNA

Yes.

DEELEY

I had a great crew in Sicily. A marvellous cameraman. Irving Shultz. Best in the business. We took a pretty austere look at the women in black. The little old women in black. I wrote the film and directed it. My name is Orson Welles.

KATE

(To ANNA.) Do you drink orange juice on your terrace in the morning, and bullshots at sunset, and look down at the sea?

ANNA

Sometimes, yes.

DEELEY

As a matter of fact I am at the top of my profession, as a matter of fact, and I have indeed been associated with substantial numbers of articulate and sensitive people, mainly prostitutes of all kinds.

KATE

(*To* ANNA.) And do you like the Sicilian people?

DEELEY

I've been there. There's nothing more to see, there's nothing more to investigate, nothing. There's nothing more in Sicily to investigate.

KATE

(*To* ANNA.) Do you like the Sicilian people?

ANNA *stares at her.*

Silence

ANNA

(*Quietly.*) Don't let's go out tonight, don't let's go anywhere tonight, let's stay in. I'll cook something, you can wash your hair, you can relax, we'll put on some records.

KATE

Oh, I don't know. We could go out.

ANNA

Why do you want to go out?

KATE

We could walk across the park.

ANNA

The park is dirty at night, all sorts of horrible people, men hiding behind trees and women with terrible voices, they scream at you as you go past, and people come out suddenly

from behind trees and bushes and there are shadows everywhere and there are policemen, and you'll have a horrible
walk, and you'll see all the traffic and the noise of the traffic and
you'll see all the hotels, and you know you hate looking
through all those swing doors, you hate it, to see all that, all
those people in the lights in the lobbies all talking and moving
. . . and all the chandeliers . . .

Pause

You'll only want to come home if you go out. You'll want to
run home . . . and into your room. . . .

Pause

KATE

What shall we do then?

ANNA

Stay in. Shall I read to you? Would you like that?

KATE

I don't know.

Pause

ANNA

Are you hungry?

KATE

No.

DEELEY

Hungry? After that casserole?

Pause

KATE

What shall I wear tomorrow? I can't make up my mind.

ANNA

Wear your green.

KATE

I haven't got the right top.

ANNA

You have. You have your turquoise blouse.

KATE

Do they go?

ANNA

Yes, they do go. Of course they go.

KATE

I'll try it.

Pause

ANNA

Would you like me to ask someone over?

KATE

Who?

ANNA

Charley . . . or Jake?

KATE

I don't like Jake.

ANNA

Well, Charley . . . or . . .

KATE

Who?

ANNA

McCabe.

Pause

KATE

I'll think about it in the bath.

ANNA

Shall I run your bath for you?

KATE

(*Standing.*) No. I'll run it myself tonight.

KATE *slowly walks to the bedroom door, goes out, closes it.*

DEELEY *stands looking at* ANNA.
ANNA *turns her head towards him.*

They look at each other.

FADE

ACT TWO

The bedroom.
A long window up centre. Door to bathroom up left. Door to sitting-room up right.

Two divans. An armchair.

The divans and armchair are disposed in precisely the same relation to each other as the furniture in the first act, but in reversed positions.

Lights dim. ANNA *discerned sitting on divan. Faint glow from glass panel in bathroom door.*

Silence.

Lights up. The other door opens. DEELEY *comes in with tray.*

DEELEY *comes into the room, places the tray on a table.*

DEELEY
Here we are. Good and hot. Good and strong and hot. You prefer it white with sugar, I believe?

ANNA
Please.

DEELEY

(*Pouring.*) Good and strong and hot with white and sugar.

He hands her the cup.

Like the room?

ANNA

Yes.

DEELEY

We sleep here. These are beds. The great thing about these beds is that they are susceptible to any amount of permutation. They can be separated as they are now. Or placed at right angles, or one can bisect the other, or you can sleep feet to feet, or head to head, or side by side. It's the castors that make all this possible.

He sits with coffee.

Yes, I remember you quite clearly from The Wayfarers.

ANNA

The what?

DEELEY

The Wayfarers Tavern, just off the Brompton Road.

ANNA

When was that?

DEELEY

Years ago.

ANNA

I don't think so.

DEELEY

Oh yes, it was you, no question. I never forget a face. You sat in the corner, quite often, sometimes alone, sometimes with others. And here you are, sitting in my house in the country. The same woman. Incredible. Fellow called Luke used to go in there. You knew him.

ANNA

Luke?

DEELEY

Big chap. Ginger hair. Ginger beard.

ANNA

I don't honestly think so.

DEELEY

Yes, a whole crowd of them, poets, stunt men, jockeys, stand-up comedians, that kind of setup. You used to wear a scarf, that's right, a black scarf, and a black sweater, and a skirt.

ANNA

Me?

DEELEY

And black stockings. Don't tell me you've forgotten The Wayfarers Tavern? You might have forgotten the name but you must remember the pub. You were the darling of the saloon bar.

ANNA

I wasn't rich, you know. I didn't have money for alcohol.

DEELEY

You had escorts. You didn't have to pay. You were looked after. I bought you a few drinks myself.

ANNA

You?

DEELEY

Sure.

ANNA

Never.

DEELEY

It's the truth. I remember clearly.

Pause

ANNA

You?

DEELEY

I've bought you drinks.

Pause

Twenty years ago . . . or so.

ANNA

You're saying we've met before?

DEELEY

Of course we've met before.

Pause

We've talked before. In that pub, for example. In the corner. Luke didn't like it much but we ignored him. Later we all went to a party. Someone's flat, somewhere in Westbourne Grove. You sat on a very low sofa, I sat opposite and looked up your skirt. Your black stockings were very black because your thighs were so white. That's something that's all over now, of course, isn't it, nothing like the same palpable profit in it now, it's all over. But it was worthwhile then. It was worthwhile that night. I simply sat sipping my light ale and gazed . . . gazed up your skirt. You didn't object, you found my gaze perfectly acceptable.

ANNA

I was aware of your gaze, was I?

DEELEY

There was a great argument going on, about China or something, or death, or China *and* death, I can't remember which, but nobody but I had a thigh-kissing view, nobody but you had the thighs which kissed. And here you are. Same woman. Same thighs.

Pause

Yes. Then a friend of yours came in, a girl, a girl friend. She sat on the sofa with you, you both chatted and chuckled, sitting together, and I settled lower to gaze at you both, at both your thighs, squealing and hissing, you aware, she unaware, but then a great multitude of men surrounded me, and demanded my opinion about death, or about China, or whatever it was, and they would not let me be but bent down over me, so that what with their stinking breath and their broken teeth and the hair in their noses and China and death and their arses on the arms of my chair I was forced to get up and plunge my way through them, followed by them with ferocity, as if I were the cause of their argument, looking back through smoke, rushing to the table with the linoleum cover to look for one more full bottle of light ale, looking back through smoke, glimpsing two girls on the sofa, one of them you, heads close, whispering, no longer able to see anything, no longer able to see stocking or thigh, and then you were gone. I wandered over to the sofa. There was no one on it. I gazed at the indentations of four buttocks. Two of which were yours.

Pause

ANNA

I've rarely heard a sadder story.

DEELEY

I agree.

ANNA

I'm terribly sorry.

DEELEY

That's all right.

Pause

I never saw you again. You disappeared from the area. Perhaps you moved out.

ANNA

No. I didn't.

DEELEY

I never saw you in The Wayfarers Tavern again. Where were you?

ANNA

Oh, at concerts, I should think, or the ballet.

Silence

Katey's taking a long time over her bath.

DEELEY

Well, you know what she's like when she gets in the bath.

ANNA

Yes.

DEELEY

Enjoys it. Takes a long time over it.

·ANNA

She does, yes.

DEELEY

A hell of a long time. Luxuriates in it. Gives herself a great
soaping all over.

Pause

Really soaps herself all over, and then washes the soap off, sud
by sud. Meticulously. She's both thorough and, I must say it,
sensuous. Gives herself a comprehensive going over, and apart
from everything else she does emerge as clean as a new pin.
Don't you think?

ANNA

Very clean.

DEELEY

Truly so. Not a speck. Not a tidemark. Shiny as a balloon.

ANNA

Yes, a kind of floating.

DEELEY

What?

ANNA

She floats from the bath. Like a dream. Unaware of anyone standing, with her towel, waiting for her, waiting to wrap it round her. Quite absorbed.

Pause

Until the towel is placed on her shoulders.

Pause

DEELEY

Of course she's so totally incompetent at drying herself properly, did you find that? She gives herself a really good *scrub*, but can she with the same efficiency give herself an equally good *rub*? I have found, in my experience of her, that this is not in fact the case. You'll always find a few odd unexpected unwanted cheeky globules dripping about.

ANNA

Why don't you dry her yourself?

DEELEY

Would you recommend that?

ANNA

You'd do it properly.

DEELEY

In her bath towel?

ANNA

How out?

DEELEY

How out?

ANNA

How could you dry her out? Out of her bath towel?

DEELEY

I don't know.

ANNA

Well, dry her yourself, in her bath towel.

Pause

DEELEY

Why don't *you* dry her in her bath towel?

ANNA

Me?

DEELEY

You'd do it properly.

ANNA

No, no.

DEELEY

Surely? I mean, you're a woman, you know how and where and in what density moisture collects on women's bodies.

ANNA

No two women are the same.

DEELEY

Well, that's true enough.

Pause

I've got a brilliant idea. Why don't we do it with powder?

ANNA

Is that a brilliant idea?

DEELEY

Isn't it?

ANNA

It's quite common to powder yourself after a bath.

DEELEY

It's quite common to powder yourself after a bath but it's quite uncommon to be powdered. Or is it? It's not common where I come from, I can tell you. My mother would have a fit.

Pause

Listen. I'll tell you what. I'll do it. I'll do the whole lot. The towel and the powder. After all, I am her husband. But you can supervise the whole thing. And give me some hot tips while you're at it. That'll kill two birds with one stone.

Pause

(*To himself.*) Christ.

He looks at her slowly.

You must be about forty, I should think, by now.

Pause

If I walked into The Wayfarers Tavern now, and saw you sitting in the corner, I wouldn't recognize you.

The bathroom door opens. KATE *comes into the bedroom. She wears a bathrobe.*

She smiles at DEELEY *and* ANNA.

KATE
(*With pleasure.*) Aaahh.

She walks to the window and looks out into the night. DEELEY *and* ANNA *watch her.*

DEELEY *begins to sing softly.*

DEELEY
(*Singing.*) The way you wear your hat . . .

ANNA
(*Singing, softly.*) The way you sip your tea . . .

DEELEY

(*Singing.*) The memory of all that . . .

ANNA

(*Singing.*) No, no, they can't take that away from me . . .

KATE *turns from the window to look at them.*

ANNA

(*Singing.*) The way your smile just beams . . .

DEELEY

(*Singing.*) The way you sing off key . . .

ANNA

(*Singing.*) The way you haunt my dreams . . .

DEELEY

(*Singing.*) No, no, they can't take that away from me . . .

KATE *walks down towards them and stands, smiling.* ANNA *and*
DEELEY *sing again, faster on cue, and more perfunctorily.*

ANNA

(*Singing.*) The way you hold your knife –

DEELEY

(*Singing.*) The way we danced till three –

ANNA

(*Singing.*) The way you've changed my life –

DEELEY

No, no, they can't take that away from me.

KATE *sits on a divan.*

ANNA

(*To* DEELEY.) Doesn't she look beautiful?

DEELEY

Doesn't she?

KATE

Thank you. I feel fresh. The water's very soft here. Much softer than London. I always find the water very hard in London. That's one reason I like living in the country. Everything's softer. The water, the light, the shapes, the sounds. There aren't such edges here. And living close to the sea too. You can't say where it begins or ends. That appeals to me. I don't care for harsh lines. I deplore that kind of urgency. I'd like to go to the East, or somewhere like that, somewhere very hot, where you can lie under a mosquito net and breathe quite slowly. You know . . . somewhere where you can look through the flap of a tent and see sand, that kind of thing. The only nice thing about a big city is that when it rains it blurs everything, and it blurs the lights from the cars, doesn't it, and blurs your eyes, and you have rain on your lashes. That's the only nice thing about a big city.

ANNA

That's not the only nice thing. You can have a nice room and a nice gas fire and a warm dressing gown and a nice hot drink, all waiting for you for when you come in.

Pause

KATE

Is it raining?

ANNA

No.

KATE

Well, I've decided I will stay in tonight anyway.

ANNA

Oh good. I am glad. Now you can have a good strong cup of coffee after your bath.

ANNA *stands, goes to coffee, pours.*

I could do the hem on your black dress. I could finish it and you could try it on.

KATE

Mmmnn.

ANNA *hands her her coffee.*

ANNA

Or I could read to you.

DEELEY

Have you dried yourself properly, Kate?

KATE

I think so.

DEELEY

Are you sure? All over?

KATE

I think so. I feel quite dry.

DEELEY

Are you quite sure? I don't want you sitting here damply all over the place.

KATE *smiles.*

See that smile? That's the same smile she smiled when I was walking down the street with her, after Odd Man Out, well, quite some time after.
What did you think of it?

ANNA

It is a very beautiful smile.

DEELEY

Do it again.

KATE

I'm still smiling.

DEELEY

You're not. Not like you were a moment ago, not like you did then.

(*To* ANNA.) You know the smile I'm talking about?

KATE

This coffee's cold.

Pause

ANNA

Oh, I'm sorry. I'll make some fresh.

KATE

No, I don't want any, thank you.

Pause

Is Charley coming?

ANNA

I can ring him if you like.

KATE

What about McCabe?

ANNA

Do you really want to see anyone?

KATE

I don't think I like McCabe.

ANNA

Nor do I.

KATE

He's strange. He says some very strange things to me.

ANNA

What things?

KATE

Oh, all sorts of funny things.

ANNA

I've never liked him.

KATE

Duncan's nice though, isn't he?

ANNA

Oh yes.

KATE

I like his poetry so much.

Pause

But you know who I like best?

ANNA

Who?

KATE

Christy.

ANNA

He's lovely.

KATE

He's so gentle, isn't he? And his humour. Hasn't he got a lovely sense of humour? And I think he's . . . so sensitive. Why don't you ask him round?

DEELEY

He can't make it. He's out of town.

KATE

Oh, what a pity.

Silence

DEELEY

(*To* ANNA.) Are you intending to visit anyone else while you're in England? Relations? Cousins? Brothers?

ANNA

No. I know no one. Except Kate.

Pause

DEELEY

Do you find her changed?.

ANNA

Oh, just a little, not very much. (*To* KATE.) You're still shy, aren't you?

KATE *stares at her.*

(*To* DEELEY.) But when I knew her first she was *so* shy, as shy as a fawn, she really was. When people leaned to speak to her she would fold away from them, so that though she was still standing within their reach she was no longer accessible to them. She folded herself from them, they were no longer able to speak or go through with their touch. I put it down to her upbringing, a parson's daughter, and indeed there was a good deal of Brontë about her.

DEELEY

Was she a parson's daughter?

ANNA

But if I thought Brontë I did not think she was Brontë in passion but only in secrecy, in being so stubbornly private.

Slight pause

I remember her first blush.

DEELEY

What? What was it? I mean why was it?

ANNA

I had borrowed some of her underwear, to go to a party. Later that night I confessed. It was naughty of me. She stared at me, nonplussed, perhaps, is the word. But I told her that in fact I had been punished for my sin, for a man at the party had spent the whole evening looking up my skirt.

Pause

DEELEY

She blushed at that?

ANNA

Deeply.

DEELEY

Looking up *your* skirt in *her* underwear. Mmnn.

ANNA

But from that night she insisted, from time to time, that I borrow her underwear – she had more of it than I, and a far greater range – and each time she proposed this she would blush, but propose it she did, nevertheless. And when there was anything to tell her, when I got back, anything of interest to tell her, I told her.

DEELEY

Did she blush then?

ANNA

I could never see then. I would come in late and find her reading under the lamp, and begin to tell her, but she would say no, turn off the light, and I would tell her in the dark. She preferred to be told in the dark. But of course it was never completely dark, what with the light from the gasfire or the light through the curtains, and what she didn't know was that, knowing her preference, I would choose a position in the room from which I could see her face, although she could not see mine. She could hear my voice only. And so she listened and I watched her listening.

DEELEY

Sounds a perfect marriage.

ANNA

We were great friends.

Pause

DEELEY

You say she was Brontë in secrecy but not in passion. What was she in passion?

ANNA

I feel that is your province.

DEELEY

You feel it's my province? Well, you're damn right. It is my province. I'm glad someone's showing a bit of taste at last. Of course it's my bloody province. I'm her husband.

Pause

I mean I'd like to ask a question. Am I alone in beginning to find all this distasteful?

ANNA

But what can you possibly find distasteful? I've flown from Rome to see my oldest friend, after twenty years, and to meet her husband. What is it that worries you?

DEELEY

What worries me is the thought of your husband rumbling about alone in his enormous villa living hand to mouth on a few hardboiled eggs and unable to speak a damn word of English.

ANNA

I interpret, when necessary.

DEELEY

Yes, but you're here, with us. He's there, alone, lurching up and down the terrace, waiting for a speedboat, waiting for a speedboat to spill out beautiful people, at least. Beautiful Mediterranean people. Waiting for all *that*, a kind of elegance we know nothing about, a slim-bellied Cote d'Azur thing we know absolutely nothing about, a lobster and lobster sauce ideology we know fuck all about, the longest legs in the world, the most phenomenally soft voices. I can hear them now. I mean let's put it on the table, I have my eye on a number of pulses, pulses all round the globe, deprivations and insults, why should I waste valuable space listening to two –

KATE

(*Swiftly.*) If you don't like it go.

Pause

DEELEY

Go? Where can I go?

KATE

To China. Or Sicily.

DEELEY

I haven't got a speedboat. I haven't got a white dinner jacket.

KATE

China then.

DEELEY

You know what they'd do to me in China if they found me in a white dinner jacket. They'd bloodywell kill me. You know what they're like over there.

Slight pause

ANNA

You are welcome to come to Sicily at any time, both of you, and be my guests.

Silence

KATE *and* DEELEY *stare at her.*

ANNA

(*To* DEELEY, *quietly.*) I would like you to understand that I came here not to disrupt but to celebrate.

Pause

To celebrate a very old and treasured friendship, something that was forged between us long before you knew of our existence.

Pause

I found her. She grew to know wonderful people, through my introduction. I took her to cafés, almost private ones, where artists and writers and sometimes actors collected, and others with dancers, and we sat hardly breathing with our coffee, listening to the life around us. All I wanted for her was her happiness. That is all I want for her still.

Pause

DEELEY

(*To* KATE.) We've met before, you know. Anna and I.

KATE *looks at him.*

Yes, we met in the Wayfarers Tavern. In the corner. She took a fancy to me. Of course I was slimhipped in those days. Pretty nifty. A bit squinky, quite honestly. Curly hair. The lot. We had a scene together. She freaked out. She didn't have any bread, so I bought her a drink. She looked at me with big eyes, shy, all that bit. She was pretending to be you at the time. Did it pretty well. Wearing your underwear she was too, at the time. Amiably allowed me a gander. Trueblue generosity. Admirable in a woman. We went to a party. Given by philosophers. Not a bad bunch. Edgware road gang. Nice lot. Haven't seen any of them for years. Old friends. Always thinking. Spoke their thoughts. Those are the people I miss. They're all dead, anyway I've never seen them again. The Maida Vale group. Big Eric and little Tony. They lived somewhere near Paddington library. On the way to the party I took her into a café, bought her a cup of coffee, beards with faces. She thought she was you, said little, so little. Maybe she was you. Maybe it was you, having coffee with me, saying little, so little.

Pause

KATE

What do you think attracted her to you?

DEELEY

I don't know. What?

KATE

She found your face very sensitive, vulnerable.

DEELEY

Did she?

KATE

She wanted to comfort it, in the way only a woman can.

DEELEY

Did she?

KATE

Oh yes.

DEELEY

She wanted to comfort my face, in the way only a woman can?

KATE

She was prepared to extend herself to you.

DEELEY

I beg your pardon?

KATE

She fell in love with you.

DEELEY

With me?

KATE

You were so unlike the others. We knew men who were brutish, crass.

DEELEY

There really are such men, then? Crass men?

KATE

Quite crass.

DEELEY

But I was crass, wasn't I, looking up her skirt?

KATE

That's not crass.

DEELEY

If it was her skirt. If it was her.

ANNA

(*Coldly.*) Oh, it was my skirt. It was me. I remember your look . . . very well. I remember you well.

KATE

(*To* ANNA.) But I remember you. I remember you dead.

Pause

I remember you lying dead. You didn't know I was watching you. I leaned over you. Your face was dirty. You lay dead, your face scrawled with dirt, all kinds of earnest inscriptions, but unblotted, so that they had run, all over your face, down to your throat. Your sheets were immaculate. I was glad. I would have been unhappy if your corpse had lain in an unwholesome sheet. It would have been graceless. I mean as far as I was concerned. As far as my room was concerned. After all, you were dead in my room. When you woke my eyes were above you, staring down at you. You tried to do my little trick, one of my tricks you had borrowed, my little slow smile, my little slow shy smile, my bend of the head, my half closing of the eyes, that we knew so well, but it didn't work, the grin only split the dirt at the sides of your mouth and stuck. You stuck in your grin. I looked for tears but could see none. Your pupils weren't in your eyes. Your bones were breaking through your face. But all was serene. There was no suffering. It had all happened elsewhere. Last rites I did not feel necessary. Or any celebration. I felt the time and season appropriate and that by dying alone and dirty you had acted with proper decorum. It was time for my bath. I had quite a lengthy bath, got out, walked about the room, glistening, drew up a chair, sat naked beside you and watched you.

Pause

When I brought him into the room your body of course had gone. What a relief it was to have a different body in my room, a male body behaving quite differently, doing all those things they do and which they think are good, like sitting with one leg over the arm of an armchair. We had a choice of two beds. Your bed or my bed. To lie in, or on. To grind noses together, in or on. He liked your bed, and thought he was different in it because he was a man. But one night I said let me do something, a little thing, a little trick. He lay there in your bed. He

looked up at me with great expectation. He was gratified. He
thought I had profited from his teaching. He thought I was
going to be sexually forthcoming, that I was about to take a
long promised initiative. I dug about in the windowbox, where
you had planted our pretty pansies, scooped, filled the bowl,
and plastered his face with dirt. He was bemused, aghast,
resisted, resisted with force. He would not let me dirty his
face, or smudge it, he wouldn't let me. He suggested a wedding instead, and a change of environment.

Slight pause

Neither mattered.

Pause

He asked me once, at about that time, who had slept in that bed
before him. I told him no one. No one at all.

Long silence

ANNA *stands, walks towards the door, stops, her back to them.*

Silence

DEELEY *starts to sob, very quietly.*

ANNA *stands still.*

ANNA *turns, switches off the lamps, sits on her divan, and lies
down.*

The sobbing stops

Silence

DEELEY *stands. He walks a few paces, looks at both divans.*

He goes to ANNA'S *divan, looks down at her. She is still.*

Silence

DEELEY *moves towards the door, stops, his back to them.*

Silence

DEELEY *turns. He goes towards* KATE'S *divan. He sits on her divan, lies across her lap.*

Long silence

DEELEY *very slowly sits up.*
He gets off the divan.
He walks slowly to the armchair.
He sits, slumped.

Silence

Lights up full sharply. Very bright.

DEELEY *in armchair.*
ANNA *lying on divan.*
KATE *sitting on divan.*

No Man's Land

No Man's Land was first presented by the National Theatre at the Old Vic, Waterloo, London, on 23rd April, 1975, with the following cast:

<table>
<tr><td>HIRST, a man in his sixties</td><td>Ralph Richardson</td></tr>
<tr><td>SPOONER, a man in his sixties</td><td>John Gielgud</td></tr>
<tr><td>FOSTER, a man in his thirties</td><td>Michael Feast</td></tr>
<tr><td>BRIGGS, a man in his forties</td><td>Terence Rigby</td></tr>
</table>

Designed by John Bury
Directed by Peter Hall

The play was subsequently presented at Wyndham's Theatre, London, from 15 July, 1975, with the same cast.

A large room in a house in North West London.
Well but sparely furnished. A strong and comfortable
straight-backed chair, in which HIRST sits.
A wall of bookshelves, with various items of pottery acting
as bookstands, including two large mugs.

Heavy curtains across the window.

The central feature of the room is an antique cabinet, with
marble top, brass gallery and open shelves, on which stands
a great variety of bottles: spirits, aperitifs, beers, etc.

Act One

Summer.

Night.

SPOONER *stands in the centre of the room.*
He is dressed in a very old and shabby suit, dark faded shirt.
creased spotted tie.

HIRST *is pouring whisky at the cabinet.*
He is precisely dressed. Sports jacket. Well cut trousers.

HIRST

As it is?

SPOONER

As it is, yes please, absolutely as it is.

HIRST *brings him the glass.*

SPOONER

Thank you. How very kind of you. How very kind.

HIRST *pours himself a vodka.*

HIRST

Cheers.

SPOONER

Your health.

They drink. SPOONER *sips.* HIRST *drinks the vodka in one gulp.*
He refills his glass, moves to his chair and sits.
SPOONER *empties his glass.*

HIRST

Please help yourself.

SPOONER

Terribly kind of you.

SPOONER goes to cabinet, pours. He turns.

SPOONER

Your good health.

He drinks.

SPOONER

What was it I was saying, as we arrived at your door?

HIRST

Ah . . . let me see.

SPOONER

Yes! I was talking about strength. Do you recall?

HIRST

Strength. Yes.

SPOONER

Yes. I was about to say, you see, that there are some people who appear to be strong, whose idea of what strength consists of is persuasive, but who inhabit the idea and not the fact. What they possess is not strength but expertise. They have nurtured and maintain what is in fact a calculated posture. Half the time it works. It takes a man of intelligence and perception to stick a needle through that posture and discern the essential flabbiness of the stance. I am such a man.

HIRST

You mean one of the latter?

SPOONER

One of the latter, yes, a man of intelligence and perception. Not one of the former, oh no, not at all. By no means.

Pause

May I say how very kind it was of you to ask me in? In fact, you are kindness itself, probably always are kindness itself, now and in England and in Hampstead and for all eternity.

He looks about the room.

What a remarkably pleasant room. I feel at peace here. Safe from all danger. But please don't be alarmed. I shan't stay long. I never stay long, with others. They do not wish it. And that, for me, is a happy state of affairs. My only security, you see, my true comfort and solace, rests in the confirmation that I elicit from people of all kinds a common and constant level of indifference. It assures me that I am as I think myself to be, that I am fixed, concrete. To show interest in me or, good gracious, anything tending towards a positive liking of me, would cause in me a condition of the acutest alarm. Fortunately, the danger is remote.

Pause

I speak to you with this startling candour because you are clearly a reticent man, which appeals, and because you are a stranger to me, and because you are clearly kindness itself.

Pause

Do you often hang about Hampstead Heath?

HIRST

No.

SPOONER

But on your excursions . . however rare . . on your rare excursions . . you hardly expect to run into the likes of me? I take it?

HIRST

Hardly.

SPOONER

I often hang about Hampstead Heath myself, expecting nothing. I'm too old for any kind of expectation. Don't you agree?

HIRST

Yes.

SPOONER

A pitfall and snare, if ever there was one. But of course I observe a good deal, on my peeps through twigs. A wit once entitled me a betwixt twig peeper. A most clumsy construction, I thought.

HIRST

Infelicitous.

SPOONER

My Christ you're right.

Pause

HIRST

What a wit.

SPOONER

You're most acutely right. All we have left is the English language. Can it be salvaged? That is my question.

HIRST

You mean in what rests its salvation?

SPOONER

More or less.

HIRST

Its salvation must rest in you.

SPOONER

It's uncommonly kind of you to say so. In you too, perhaps, although I haven't sufficient evidence to go on, as yet.

Pause

HIRST

You mean because I've said little?

SPOONER

You're a quiet one. It's a great relief. Can you imagine two of us gabbling away like me? It would be intolerable.

Pause

By the way, with reference to peeping, I do feel it incumbent upon me to make one thing clear. I don't peep on sex. That's gone forever. You follow me? When my twigs happen to shall I say rest their peep on sexual conjugations, however periphrastic, I see only whites of eyes, so close, they glut me, no distance possible, and when you can't keep the proper distance between yourself and others, when you can no longer maintain an objective relation to matter, the game's not worth the candle, so forget it and remember that what is obligatory to keep in your vision is space, space in moonlight particularly, and lots of it.

HIRST

You speak with the weight of experience behind you.

SPOONER

And beneath me. Experience is a paltry thing. Everyone has it and will tell his tale of it. I leave experience to psychological interpreters, the wetdream world. I myself can do any graph of experience you wish, to suit your taste or mine. Child's play. The present will not be distorted. I am a poet. I am interested in where I am eternally present and active.

HIRST *stands, goes to cabinet, pours vodka.*

I have gone too far, you think?

HIRST

I'm expecting you to go very much further.

SPOONER

Really? That doesn't mean I interest you, I hope?

HIRST

Not in the least.

SPOONER

Thank goodness for that. For a moment my heart sank.

HIRST *draws the curtains aside, looks out briefly, lets curtain fall, remains standing.*

But nevertheless you're right. Your instinct is sound. I could go further, in more ways than one. I could advance, reserve my defences, throw on a substitute, call up the cavalry, or throw everything forward out of the knowledge that when joy over-

floweth there can be no holding of joy. The point I'm trying
to make, in case you've missed it, is that I am a free man.

HIRST *pours himself another vodka and drinks it. He puts the
glass down, moves carefully to his chair, sits.*

                    HIRST
It's a long time since we had a free man in this house.

                    SPOONER
We?

                    HIRST
I.

                    SPOONER
Is there another?

                    HIRST
Another what?

                    SPOONER
People. Person.

                    HIRST
What other?

                    SPOONER
There are two mugs on that shelf.

                    HIRST
The second is for you.

SPOONER

And the first?

HIRST

Would you like to use it? Would you like some hot refreshment?

SPOONER

That would be dangerous. I'll stick to your scotch, if I may.

HIRST

Help yourself.

SPOONER

Thank you.

He goes to cabinet.

HIRST

I'll take a whisky with you, if you would be so kind.

SPOONER

With pleasure. Weren't you drinking vodka?

HIRST

I'll be happy to join you in a whisky.

SPOONER *pours.*

SPOONER

You'll take it as it is, as it comes?

HIRST

Oh, absolutely as it comes.

SPOONER *brings* HIRST *his glass.*

SPOONER

Your very good health.

HIRST

Yours.

They drink.

Tell me . . . do you often hang about Jack Straw's Castle?

SPOONER

I knew it as a boy.

HIRST

Do you find it as beguiling a public house now as it was in the days of the highwaymen, when it was frequented by highway-men? Notably Jack Straw. The great Jack Straw. Do you find it much changed?

SPOONER

It changed my life.

HIRST

Good Lord. Did it really?

SPOONER

I refer to a midsummer night, when I shared a drink with a Hungarian émigré, lately retired from Paris.

HIRST

The same drink?

SPOONER

By no means. You've guessed, I would imagine, that he was an erstwhile member of the Hungarian aristocracy?

HIRST

I did guess, yes.

SPOONER

On that summer evening, led by him, I first appreciated how quiet life can be, in the midst of yahoos and hullabaloos. He exerted on me a quite uniquely . . . calming influence, without exertion, without any . . . desire to influence. He was so much older than me. My expectations in those days, and I confess I had expectations in those days, did not include him in their frame of reference. I'd meandered over to Hampstead Heath, a captive to memories of a more than usually pronounced grisliness, and found myself, not much to my surprise, ordering a pint at the bar of Jack Straw's Castle. This achieved, and having negotiated a path through a particularly repellent lick-spittling herd of literati, I stumbled, unseeing, with my pint, to his bald, tanned, unmoving table. How bald he was.

Pause

I think, after quite half my pint had descended, never to be savoured again, that I spoke, suddenly, suddenly spoke, and received . . . a response, no other word will do, a response, the like of which –

HIRST

What was he drinking?

SPOONER

What?

HIRST

What was he drinking?

SPOONER

Pernod.

Pause

I was impressed, more or less at that point, by an intuition that he possessed a measure of serenity the like of which I had never encountered.

HIRST

What did he say?

SPOONER *stares at him.*

SPOONER

You expect me to remember what he said?

HIRST

No.

Pause

SPOONER

What he said . . . all those years ago . . . is neither here nor there. It was not what he said but possibly the way he sat which has remained with me all my life and has, I am quite sure, made me what I am.

Pause

And I met you at the same pub tonight, although at a different table.

Pause

And I wonder at you, now, as once I wondered at him. But will I wonder at you tomorrow, I wonder, as I still wonder at him today?

HIRST

I cannot say.

SPOONER

It cannot be said.

Pause

I'll ask you another question. Have you any idea from what I derive my strength?

HIRST

Strength? No.

SPOONER

I have never been loved. From this I derive my strength. Have you? Ever? Been loved?

HIRST

Oh, I don't suppose so.

SPOONER

I looked up once into my mother's face. What I saw there was nothing less than pure malevolence. I was fortunate to escape with my life. You will want to know what I had done to provoke such hatred in my own mother.

HIRST

You'd pissed yourself.

SPOONER

Quite right. How old do you think I was at the time?

HIRST

Twenty eight.

SPOONER

Quite right. However, I left home soon after.

Pause

My mother remains, I have to say, a terribly attractive woman in many ways. Her buns are the best.

HIRST *looks at him.*

Her currant buns. The best.

HIRST

Would you be so kind as to pour me another drop of whisky?

SPOONER

Certainly.

SPOONER *takes the glass, pours whisky into it, gives it to* HIRST.

SPOONER

Perhaps it's about time I introduced myself. My name is Spooner.

HIRST

Ah.

SPOONER

I'm a staunch friend of the arts, particularly the art of poetry, and a guide to the young. I keep open house. Young poets come to me. They read me their verses. I comment, give them coffee, make no charge. Women are admitted, some of whom are also poets. Some are not. Some of the men are not. Most of the men are not. But with the windows open to the garden, my wife pouring long glasses of squash, with ice, on a summer evening, young voices occasionally lifted in unaccompanied ballad, young bodies lying in the dying light, my wife moving through the shadows in her long gown, what can ail? I mean who can gainsay us? What quarrel can be found with what is, *au fond*, a gesture towards the sustenance and preservation of art, and through art to virtue?

HIRST

Through art to virtue. (*Raises glass.*) To your continued health.

SPOONER *sits, for the first time.*

SPOONER

When we had our cottage . . . when we had our cottage . . . we gave our visitors tea, on the lawn.

HIRST

I did the same.

SPOONER

On the lawn?

HIRST

I did the same.

SPOONER

You had a cottage?

HIRST

Tea on the lawn.

SPOONER

What happened to them? What happened to our cottages?
What happened to our lawns?

Pause

Be frank. Tell me. You've revealed something. You've made an
unequivocal reference to your past. Don't go back on it. We
share something. A memory of the bucolic life. We're both
English.

Pause

HIRST

In the village church, the beams are hung with garlands, in
honour of young women of the parish, reputed to have died
virgin.

Pause

However, the garlands are not bestowed on maidens only, but
on all who die unmarried, wearing the white flower of a blame-
less life.

Pause

SPOONER

You mean that not only young women of the parish but also
young men of the parish are so honoured?

HIRST

I do.

SPOONER

And that old men of the parish who also died maiden are so garlanded?

HIRST

Certainly.

SPOONER

I am enraptured. Tell me more. Tell me more about the quaint little perversions of your life and times. Tell me more, with all the authority and brilliance you can muster, about the socio-politico-economic structure of the environment in which you attained to the age of reason. Tell me more.

Pause

HIRST

There is no more.

SPOONER

Tell me then about your wife.

HIRST

What wife?

SPOONER

How beautiful she was, how tender and how true. Tell me with what speed she swung in the air, with what velocity she came off the wicket, whether she was responsive to finger spin, whether you could bowl a shooter with her, or an offbreak with a legbreak action. In other words, did she google?

Silence

You will not say. I will tell you then . . . that my wife . . . had everything. Eyes, a mouth, hair, teeth, buttocks, breasts, absolutely everything. And legs.

HIRST

Which carried her away.

SPOONER

Carried who away? Yours or mine?

Pause

Is she here now, your wife? Cowering in a locked room, perhaps?

Pause

Was she ever here? Was she ever there, in your cottage? It is my duty to tell you you have failed to convince. I am an honest and intelligent man. You pay me less than my due. Are you, equally, being fair to the lady? I begin to wonder whether truly accurate and therefore essentially poetic definition means anything to you at all. I begin to wonder whether you do in fact truly remember her, whether you truly did love her, truly caressed her, truly did cradle her, truly did husband her, falsely dreamed or did truly adore her. I have seriously questioned these propositions and find them threadbare.

Silence

Her eyes, I take it, were hazel?

HIRST *stands, carefully. He moves, with a slight stagger, to the cabinet, pours whisky, drinks.*

HIRST

Hazel shit.

SPOONER

Good lord, good lord, do I detect a touch of the maudlin?

Pause

Hazel shit. I ask myself: Have I ever seen hazel shit? Or hazel eyes, for that matter?

HIRST *throws his glass at him, ineffectually. It bounces on the carpet.*

Do I detect a touch of the hostile? Do I detect – with respect – a touch of too many glasses of ale followed by the great malt which wounds? Which wounds?

Silence

HIRST

Tonight . . . my friend . . . you find me in the last lap of a race . . . I had long forgotten to run.

Pause

SPOONER

A metaphor. Things are looking up.

Pause

I would say, albeit on a brief acquaintance, that you lack the essential quality of manliness, which is to put your money

where your mouth is, to pick up a pintpot and know it to be a
pintpot, and knowing it to be a pintpot, to declare it as a pintpot, and to stay faithful to that pintpot as though you had given
birth to it out of your own arse. You lack that capability, in my
view.

Pause

Do forgive me my candour. It is not method but madness. So
you won't, I hope, object if I take out my prayer beads and
my prayer mat and salute what I take to be your impotence?

He stands.

I salute. And attend. And saluting and attending am at your
service all embracing. Heed me. I am a relevant witness. And
could be a friend.

HIRST *grips the cabinet, rigid.*

You need a friend, You have a long hike, my lad, up which,
presently, you slog unfriended. Let me perhaps be your boat-
man. For if and when we talk of a river we talk of a deep and
dank architecture. In other words, never disdain a helping
hand, especially one of such rare quality. And it is not only the
quality of my offer which is rare, it is the act itself, the offer
itself – quite without precedent. I offer myself to you as a
friend. Think before you speak.

HIRST *attempts to move, stops, grips the cabinet.*

Remember this. You've lost your wife of hazel hue, you've lost her and what can you do, she will no more come back to you, with a tillifola tillifola tillifoladi-foladi-foloo.

HIRST

No.

Pause

No man's land . . . does not move . . . or change . . . or grow old . . . remains . . . forever . . . icy . . . silent.

HIRST *loosens his grip on the cabinet, staggers, across the room, holds on to a chair.*

He waits, moves, falls.

He waits, gets to his feet, moves, falls.

SPOONER *watches.*

HIRST *crawls towards the door, manages to open it, crawls out of the door.*

SPOONER *remains still.*

SPOONER

I have known this before. The exit through the door, by way of belly and floor.

He looks at the room, walks about it, looking at each object closely, stops, hands behind his back, surveying the room.

A door, somewhere in the house, closes.

Silence.

The front door opens, and slams sharply.

SPOONER *stiffens, is still.*

FOSTER *enters the room. He is casually dressed.*

He stops still upon seeing SPOONER. *He stands, looking at* SPOONER.

Silence

FOSTER

What are you drinking? Christ I'm thirsty. How are you? I'm parched.

He goes to cabinet, opens a bottle of beer, pours.

What are you drinking? It's bloody late. I'm worn to a frazzle. This is what I want. (*He drinks.*) Taxi? No chance. Taxi drivers are against me. Something about me. Some unknown factor. My gait, perhaps. Or perhaps because I travel incognito. Oh, that's better. Works wonders. How are you? What are you drinking? Who are you? I thought I'd never make it. What a hike. And not only that. I'm defenceless. I don't carry a gun in London. But I'm not bothered. Once you've done the East you've done it all. I've done the East. But I still like a nice lighthouse like this one. Have you met your host? He's my father. It was our night off tonight, you see. He was going to stay at home, listen to some lieder. I hope he had a quiet and pleasant evening. Who are you, by the way? What are you drinking?

SPOONER

I'm a friend of his.

FOSTER

You're not typical.

BRIGGS *comes into the room, stops. He is casually dressed, stocky.*

BRIGGS

Who's this?

FOSTER

His name's Friend. This is Mr. Briggs. Mr. Friend – Mr. Briggs. I'm Mr. Foster. Old English stock. John Foster. Jack. Jack Foster. Old English name. Foster. John Foster. Jack Foster. Foster. This man's name is Briggs.

Pause

BRIGGS

I've seen Mr. Friend before.

FOSTER

Seen him before?

BRIGGS

I know him.

FOSTER

Do you really?

BRIGGS

I've seen you before.

SPOONER

Possibly, possibly.

BRIGGS

Yes. You collect the beermugs from the tables in a pub in Chalk Farm.

SPOONER

The landlord's a friend of mine. When he's shorthanded, I give him a helping hand.

BRIGGS

Who says the landlord's a friend of yours?

FOSTER

He does.

BRIGGS

I'm talking about The Bull's Head in Chalk Farm.

SPOONER

Yes, yes. So am I.

BRIGGS

So am I.

FOSTER

I know The Bull's Head. The landlord's a friend of mine.

BRIGGS

He collects the mugs.

FOSTER

A firstclass pub. I've known the landlord for years.

BRIGGS

He says he's a friend of the landlord.

FOSTER

He says he's a friend of our friend too.

BRIGGS

What friend?

FOSTER

Our host.

BRIGGS

He's a bloody friend of everyone then.

FOSTER

He's everybody's bloody friend. How many friends have you got altogether, Mr. Friend?

BRIGGS

He probably couldn't count them.

FOSTER

Well, there's me too, now. I'm another one of your new friends. I'm your newest new friend. Not him. Not Briggs. He's nobody's fucking friend. People tend to be a little wary of Briggs. They balk at giving him their all. But me they like at first sight.

BRIGGS

Sometimes they love you at first sight.

FOSTER

Sometimes they do. That's why, when I travel, I get all the gold, nobody offers me dross. People take an immediate shine to me, especially women, especially in Siam or Bali. He knows I'm not a liar. Tell him about the Siamese girls.

BRIGGS

They loved him at first sight.

FOSTER

(*To* SPOONER.) You're not Siamese though, are you?

BRIGGS

He's a very long way from being Siamese.

FOSTER

Ever been out there?

SPOONER

I've been to Amsterdam.

FOSTER *and* BRIGGS *stare at him.*

I mean that was the last place . . . I visited. I know Europe well. My name is Spooner, by the way. Yes, one afternoon in Amsterdam . . . I was sitting outside a café by a canal. The weather was superb. At another table, in shadow, was a man whistling under his breath, sitting very still, almost rigid. At the side of the canal was a fisherman. He caught a fish. He lifted it high. The waiter cheered and applauded, the two men, the waiter and the fisherman, laughed. A little girl, passing, laughed. Two lovers, passing, kissed. The fish was lofted, on the rod. The fish and the rod glinted in the sun, as they swayed. The fisherman's cheeks were flushed, with pleasure. I decided to paint a picture – of the canal, the waiter, the child, the fisherman, the lovers, the fish, and in background, in shadow, the man at the other table, and to call it The Whistler. The Whistler. If you had seen the picture, and the title, would the title have baffled you?

Pause

FOSTER

(*To* BRIGGS.) Do you want to answer that question?

BRIGGS

No. Go on. You answer it.

FOSTER

Well, speaking for myself, I think I would have been baffled by that title. But I might have appreciated the picture. I might even have been grateful for it.

Pause

Did you hear what I said? I might have been grateful for the picture. A good work of art tends to move me. You follow me? I'm not a cunt, you know.

Pause

I'm very interested to hear you're a painter. You do it in your spare time, I suppose?

SPOONER

Quite.

FOSTER

Did you ever paint that picture, The Whistler?

SPOONER

Not yet, I'm afraid.

FOSTER

Don't leave it too long. You might lose the inspiration.

BRIGGS

Ever painted a beermug?

SPOONER

You must come and see my collection, any time you wish.

BRIGGS

What of, beermugs?

SPOONER

No, no. Paintings.

FOSTER

Where do you keep it?

SPOONER

At my house in the country. You would receive the warmest of welcomes.

FOSTER

Who from?

SPOONER

My wife. My two daughters.

FOSTER

Really? Would they like me? What do you think? Would they love me at first sight?

SPOONER

(*Laughing.*) Quite possibly.

FOSTER

What about him?

SPOONER *looks at* BRIGGS.

SPOONER

They are remarkably gracious women.

FOSTER

You're a lucky man. What are you drinking?

SPOONER

Scotch.

FOSTER *goes to cabinet, pours scotch, stands holding glass.*

FOSTER

What do you make of this? When I was out East . . . once . . a kind of old stinking tramp, bollock naked, asked me for a few bob. I didn't know him. He was a complete stranger. But I could see immediately he wasn't a man to trust. He had a dog with him. They only had about one eye between them. So I threw him some sort of coin. He caught this bloody coin, looked at it with a bit of disaste, and then he threw the coin back. Well, automatically I went to catch it, I clutched at it, but the bloody coin disappeared into thin air. It didn't drop anywhere. It just disappeared . . into thin air . . on its way towards me. He then let out a few curses and pissed off, with his dog. Oh, here's your whisky, by the way. (*Hands it to him.*) What do you make of that incident?

SPOONER

He was a con artist.

FOSTER

Do you think so?

SPOONER

You would be wise to grant the event no integrity whatsoever.

FOSTER

You don't subscribe to the mystery of the Orient?

SPOONER

A typical Eastern contrick.

FOSTER

Double Dutch, you mean?

SPOONER

Certainly. Your good health. (*Drinks*.)

HIRST *enters, wearing a dressing-gown.*

BRIGGS *goes to cabinet, pours whisky.*

HIRST

I can't sleep. I slept briefly. I think. Perhaps it was sufficient. Yes. I woke up, out of a dream. I feel cheerful. Who'll give me a glass of whisky?

HIRST *sits.* BRIGGS *brings him whisky.*

My goodness, is this for me? How did you know? You knew. You're very sensitive. Cheers. The first today. What day is it? What's the time? Is it still night?

BRIGGS

Yes.

HIRST

The same night? I was dreaming of a waterfall. No, no, of a lake. I think it was . . just recently. Can you remember when I went to bed? Was it daylight? It's good to go to sleep in the

late afternoon. After tea and toast. You hear the faint begin-
nings of the evening sounds, and then nothing. Everywhere
else people are changing for dinner. You're tucked up, the
shutters closed, gaining a march on the world.

He passes his glass to BRIGGS, *who fills and returns it.*

Something is depressing me. What is it? It was the dream, yes.
Waterfalls. No, no, a lake. Water. Drowning. Not me. Someone else. How nice to have company. Can you imagine waking
up, finding no-one here, just furniture, staring at you? Most
unpleasant. I've known that condition, I've been through that
period – cheers – I came round to human beings in the end.
Like yourselves. A wise move. I tried laughing alone. Pathetic.
Have you all got drinks?

He looks at SPOONER.

Who's that? A friend of yours? Won't someone introduce me?

FOSTER

He's a friend of yours.

HIRST

In the past I knew remarkable people. I've a photograph album
somewhere. I'll find it. You'll be impressed by the faces. Very
handsome. Sitting on grass with hampers. I had a moustache.
Quite a few of my friends had moustaches. Remarkable faces.
Remarkable moustaches. What was it informed the scene?
A tenderness towards our fellows, perhaps. The sun shone. The
girls had lovely hair, dark, sometimes red. Under their dresses
their bodies were white. It's all in my album. I'll find it. You'll
be struck by the charm of the girls, their grace, the ease with
which they sit, pour tea, loll. It's all in my album.

He empties glass, holds it up.

Who is the kindest among you?

BRIGGS *takes glass to cabinet.*

Thank you. What would I do without the two of you? I'd sit here forever, waiting for a stranger to fill up my glass. What would I do while I waited? Look through my album? Make plans for the future?

BRIGGS
(*Bringing glass.*) You'd crawl to the bottle and stuff it between your teeth.

HIRST
No. I drink with dignity.

He drinks, looks at SPOONER.

Who is this man? Do I know him?

FOSTER
He says he's a friend of yours.

HIRST
My true friends look out at me from my album. I had my world. I have it. Don't think now that it's gone I'll choose to sneer at it, to cast doubt on it, to wonder if it properly existed. No. We're talking of my youth, which can never leave me. No. It existed. It was solid, the people in it were solid, while . . . transformed by light, while being sensitive . . . to all the changing light.

When I stood my shadow fell upon her. She looked up.
Give me the bottle. Give me the bottle.

BRIGGS *gives him the bottle. He drinks from it.*

It's gone. Did it exist? It's gone. It never existed. It remains.

I am sitting here forever.

How kind of you. I wish you'd tell me what the weather's
like. I wish you'd damnwell tell me what night it is, this night
or the next night or the other one, the night before last. Be
frank. Is it the night before last?

Help yourselves. I hate drinking alone. There's too much
solitary shittery.

What was it? Shadows. Brightness, through leaves. Gam-
bolling. In the bushes. Young lovers. A fall of water. It was my
dream. The lake. Who was drowning in my dream?

It was blinding. I remember it. I've forgotten. By all that's
sacred and holy. The sounds stopped. It was freezing. There's a
gap in me. I can't fill it. There's a flood running through me.
I can't plug it. They're blotting me out. Who is doing it? I'm
suffocating. It's a muff. A muff, perfumed. Someone is doing
me to death.

She looked up. I was staggered. I had never seen anything so
beautiful. That's all poison. We can't be expected to live like
that.

I remember nothing. I'm sitting in this room. I see you all,
every one of you. A sociable gathering. The dispositions are
kindly.

Am I asleep? There's no water. No-one is drowning.

Yes, yes, come on, come on, come on, pipe up, speak up, speak up, speak up, you're fucking me about, you bastards, ghosts, long ghosts, you're making noises, I can hear you humming, I wear a crisp blue shirt at the Ritz, I wear a crisp blue shirt at the Ritz, I know him well, the wine waiter, Boris, Boris, he's been there for years, blinding shadows, then a fall of water –

SPOONER

It was I drowning in your dream.

HIRST *falls to the floor. They all go to him.*
FOSTER *turns to* SPOONER.

FOSTER

Bugger off.

BRIGGS *pulls* HIRST *up.* HIRST *wards him off.*

HIRST

Unhand me.

He stands erect. SPOONER *moves to him.*

SPOONER

He has grandchildren. As have I. As I have. We both have fathered. We are of an age. I know his wants. Let me take his arm. Respect our age. Come, I'll seat you.

He takes HIRST's *arm and leads him to a chair.*

There's no pity in these people.

FOSTER

Christ.

SPOONER

I am your true friend. That is why your dream . . . was so distressing. You saw me drowning in your dream. But have no fear. I am not drowned.

FOSTER

Christ.

SPOONER

(*To* HIRST.) Would you like me to make you some coffee?

BRIGGS

He thinks he's a waiter in Amsterdam.

FOSTER

Service non compris.

BRIGGS

Whereas he's a pintpot attendant in The Bull's Head. And a pisspot attendant as well.

FOSTER

Our host must have been in The Bull's Head tonight, where he had an unfortunate encounter. (*To* SPOONER.) Hey scout, I think there's been some kind of misunderstanding. You're not in some shithouse down by the docks. You're in the home of a man of means, of a man of achievement. Do you understand me?

He turns to BRIGGS.

Why am I bothering? Tell me. Eh?

He turns back to SPOONER.

Listen chummybum. We protect this gentleman against corruption, against men of craft, against men of evil, we could destroy you without a glance, we take care of this gentleman, we do it out of love.

He turns to BRIGGS.

Why am I talking to him? I'm wasting my time with a non-starter. I must be going mad. I don't usually talk. I don't have to. Normally I keep quiet.

He turns back to SPOONER.

I know what it is. There's something about you fascinates me.

SPOONER

It's my bearing.

FOSTER

That's what it must be.

BRIGGS

I've seen Irishmen chop his balls off.

FOSTER

I suppose once you've had Irishmen you've had everything. (*To* SPOONER.) Listen. Keep it tidy. You follow? You've just laid your hands on a rich and powerful man. It's not what you're used to, scout. How can I make it clear? This is another class. It's another realm of operation. It's a world of silk. It's a world of organdie. It's a world of flower arrangements. It's a world of eighteenth century cookery books. It's nothing to do with toffeeapples and a packet of crisps. It's milk in the bath. It's the cloth bellpull. It's organisation.

BRIGGS

It's not rubbish.

FOSTER

It's not rubbish. We deal in originals. Nothing duff, nothing
ersatz, we don't open any old bottle of brandy. Mind you
don't fall into a quicksand. (*To* BRIGGS.) Why don't I kick his
head off and have done with it?

SPOONER

I'm the same age as your master. I used to picnic in the
country too, at the same time as he.

FOSTER

Listen, my friend. This man in this chair, he's a creative man.
He's an artist. We make life possible for him. We're in a
position of trust. Don't try to drive a wedge into a happy
household. You understand me? Don't try to make a nonsense
out of family life.

BRIGGS

(*To* FOSTER.) If you can't, I can.

He moves to SPOONER *and beckons to him, with his forefinger.*

BRIGGS

Come here.

HIRST

Where are the sandwiches? Cut the bread.

BRIGGS

It's cut.

HIRST

It is not cut. Cut it!

BRIGGS *stands still.*

BRIGGS

I'll go and cut it.

He leaves the room.

HIRST

(*To* SPOONER.) I know you from somewhere.

FOSTER

I must clean the house. No-one else'll do it. Your financial adviser is coming to breakfast. I've got to think about that. His taste changes from day to day. One day he wants boiled eggs and toast, the next day orange juice and poached eggs, the next scrambled eggs and smoked salmon, the next a mushroom omelette and champagne. Any minute now it'll be dawn. A new day. Your financial adviser's dreaming of his breakfast. He's dreaming of eggs. Eggs, eggs. What kind of eggs? I'm exhausted. I've been up all night. But it never stops. Nothing stops. It's all fizz. This is my life. I have my brief arousals. They leave me panting. I can't take the pace in London. Nobody knows what I miss.

BRIGGS *enters and stands, listening.*

I miss the Siamese girls. I miss the girls in Bali. You don't come across them over here. You see them occasionally, on the steps of language schools, they're learning English, they're not prepared to have a giggle and a cuddle in their own language. Not in Regent street. A giggle and a cuddle. Sometimes my ambitions extend no further than that. I could do something else. I could make another life. I don't have to waste my time looking after a pisshound. I could find the right niche and be happy. The right niche, the right happiness.

BRIGGS

We're out of bread. I'm looking at the housekeeper. Neurotic poof. He prefers idleness. Unspeakable ponce. He prefers the Malay Straits, where they give you hot toddy in a fourposter. He's nothing but a vagabond cock. (*To* SPOONER.) Move over.

SPOONER *moves out of his way.*

BRIGGS

(*To* HIRST.) Get up.

HIRST *slowly stands.* BRIGGS *leads him to the door.*

BRIGGS

(*To* HIRST.) Keep on the move. Don't look back.

HIRST

I know that man.

BRIGGS *leads* HIRST *out of the room.*

Silence

FOSTER

Do you know what I saw once in the desert, in the Australian desert? A man walking along carrying two umbrellas. Two umbrellas. In the outback.

Pause

SPOONER

Was it raining?

FOSTER

No. It was a beautiful day. I nearly asked him what he was up to but I changed my mind.

SPOONER

Why?

FOSTER

Well, I decided he must be some kind of lunatic. I thought he would only confuse me.

FOSTER *walks about the room, stops at the door.*

Listen. You know what it's like when you're in a room with the light on and then suddenly the light goes out? I'll show you. It's like this.

He turns the light out.

BLACKOUT

Act Two

Morning

SPOONER *is alone in the room. The curtains are still closed, but shafts of light enter the room.*

He is sitting.

He stands, goes slowly to door, tries handle, with fatigue, withdraws.

SPOONER

I have known this before. Morning. A locked door. A house of silence and strangers.

He sits, shivers.

The door is unlocked. BRIGGS *comes in, key in hand. He is wearing a suit. He opens the curtains. Daylight.*

BRIGGS

I've been asked to inquire if you're hungry.

SPOONER

Food? I never touch it.

BRIGGS

The financial adviser didn't turn up. You can have his breakfast. He phoned his order through, then phoned again to cancel the appointment.

SPOONER

For what reason?

BRIGGS

Jack spoke to him, not me.

SPOONER

What reason did he give your friend?

BRIGGS

Jack said he said he found himself without warning in the centre of a vast aboriginal financial calamity.

Pause

SPOONER

He clearly needs an adviser.

Pause

BRIGGS

I won't bring you breakfast if you're going to waste it.

SPOONER

I abhor waste.

BRIGGS *goes out.*

I have known this before. The door unlocked. The entrance of a stranger. The offer of alms. The shark in the harbour.

Silence

BRIGGS *enters carrying a tray. On the tray are breakfast dishes covered by silver lids and a bottle of champagne in a bucket.*

He places the tray on a small table and brings a chair to the table.

BRIGGS

Scrambled eggs. Shall I open the champagne?

SPOONER

Is it cold?

BRIGGS

Freezing.

SPOONER

Please open it.

BRIGGS *begins to open bottle.* SPOONER *lifts lids, peers, sets lids aside, butters toast.*

SPOONER

Who is the cook?

BRIGGS

We share all burdens, Jack and myself.

BRIGGS *pours champagne. Offers glass.* SPOONER *sips.*

Pause

SPOONER

Thank you.

SPOONER *begins to eat.* BRIGGS *draws up a chair to the table and sits, watching.*

BRIGGS

We're old friends, Jack and myself. We met at a street corner. I should tell you he'll deny this account. His story will be different. I was standing at a street corner. A car drew up. It was him. He asked me the way to Bolsover street. I told him Bolsover street was in the middle of an intricate one-way system. It was a one-way system easy enough to get into. The only trouble was that, once in, you couldn't get out. I told him his best bet, if he really wanted to get to Bolsover street, was to take the first left, first right, second right, third on the left, keep his eye open for a hardware shop, go right round the square, keeping to the inside lane, take the second Mews on the right and then stop. He will find himself facing a very tall office block, with a crescent courtyard. He can take advantage of this office block. He can go round the crescent, come out the other way, follow the arrows, go past two sets of traffic lights and take the next left indicated by the first green filter he comes across. He's got the Post Office Tower in his vision the whole time. All he's got to do is to reverse into the underground car park, change gear, go straight on, and he'll find himself in Bolsover street with no trouble at all. I did warn him, though, that he'll still be faced with the problem, having found Bolsover street, of losing it. I told him I knew one or two people who'd been wandering up and down Bolsover street for years. They'd wasted their bloody youth there. The people who live there, their faces are grey, they're in a state of despair, but nobody pays any attention, you see. All people are worried about is their illgotten gains. I wrote to The Times about it. Life At A Dead End, I called it. Went for nothing. Anyway, I told him that probably the best thing he could do was to forget the whole idea of getting to Bolsover street. I remember saying to him: This trip you've got in mind, drop it, it could prove fatal. But he said he had to deliver a parcel. Anyway, I took all this trouble with him because he had a nice open face.

He looked like a man who would always do good to others himself. Normally I wouldn't give a fuck. I should tell you he'll deny this account. His story will be different.

SPOONER *places the lid on his plate.*

BRIGGS *pours champagne into* SPOONER's *glass.*

When did you last have champagne for breakfast?

SPOONER
Well, to be quite honest, I'm a champagne drinker.

BRIGGS
Oh, are you?

SPOONER
I know my wines. (*He drinks.*) Dijon. In the thirties. I made many trips to Dijon, for the winetasting, with my French translator. Even after his death, I continued to go to Dijon, until I could go no longer.

Pause

Hugo. A good companion.

Pause.

You will wonder of course what he translated. The answer is my verse. I am a poet.

Pause

BRIGGS
I thought poets were young.

SPOONER

I am young. (*He reaches for the bottle.*) Can I help you to a glass?

BRIGGS

No, thank you.

SPOONER *examines the bottle.*

SPOONER

An excellent choice.

BRIGGS

Not mine.

SPOONER

(*Pouring.*) Translating verse is an extremely difficult task. Only the Rumanians remain respectable exponents of the craft.

BRIGGS

Bit early in the morning for all this, isn't it?

SPOONER *drinks.*

Finish the bottle. Doctor's orders.

SPOONER

Can I enquire as to why I was locked in this room, by the way?

BRIGGS

Doctor's orders.

Pause

Tell me when you're ready for coffee.

Pause

It must be wonderful to be a poet and to have admirers. And translators. And to be young. I'm neither one nor the other.

SPOONER

Yes. You've reminded me. I must be off. I have a meeting at twelve. Thank you so much for breakfast.

BRIGGS

What meeting?

SPOONER

A board meeting. I'm on the board of a recently inaugurated poetry magazine. We have our first meeting at twelve. Can't be late.

BRIGGS

Where's the meeting?

SPOONER

At The Bull's Head in Chalk Farm. The landlord is kindly allowing us the use of a private room on the first floor. It is essential that the meeting be private, you see, as we shall be discussing policy.

BRIGGS

The Bull's Head in Chalk Farm?

SPOONER

Yes. The landlord is a friend of mine. It is on that account that he has favoured us with a private room. It is true of course that I informed him Lord Lancer would be attending the meeting. He at once appreciated that a certain degree of sequesteredness would be the order of the day.

BRIGGS

Lord Lancer?

SPOONER

Our patron.

BRIGGS

He's not one of the Bengal Lancers, is he?

SPOONER

No, no. He's of Norman descent.

BRIGGS

A man of culture?

SPOONER

Impeccable credentials.

BRIGGS

Some of these aristocrats hate the arts.

SPOONER

Lord Lancer is a man of honour. He loves the arts. He has declared this love in public. He never goes back on his word. But I must be off. Lord Lancer does not subscribe to the view that poets can treat time with nonchalance.

BRIGGS

Jack could do with a patron.

SPOONER

Jack?

BRIGGS

He's a poet.

SPOONER

A poet? Really? Well, if he'd like to send me some examples of his work, double spaced on quarto, with copies in a separate folder by separate post in case of loss or misappropriation, stamped addressed envelope enclosed, I'll read them.

BRIGGS

That's very nice of you.

SPOONER

Not at all. You can tell him he can look forward to a scrupulously honest and, if I may say so, highly sensitive judgement.

BRIGGS

I'll tell him. He's in real need of a patron. The boss could be his patron, but he's not interested. Perhaps because he's a poet himself. It's possible there's an element of jealousy in it, I don't know. Not that the boss isn't a very kind man. He is. He's a very civilised man. But he's still human.

Pause

SPOONER

The boss . . . is a poet himself?

BRIGGS

Don't be silly. He's more than that, isn't he? He's an essayist and critic as well. He's a man of letters.

SPOONER

I thought his face was familiar.

The telephone buzzes. BRIGGS *goes to it, lifts it, listens.*

BRIGGS

Yes, sir.

BRIGGS *picks up the tray and takes it out.*

SPOONER *sits still.*

SPOONER

I have known this before. The voice unheard. A listener.
The command from an upper floor.

He pours champagne.

HIRST *enters, wearing a suit, followed by* BRIGGS.

HIRST

Charles. How nice of you to drop in.

He shakes SPOONER's *hand.*

Have they been looking after you all right? Denson, let's have
some coffee.

BRIGGS *leaves the room.*

You're looking remarkably well. Haven't changed a bit. It's
the squash, I expect. Keeps you up to the mark. You were
quite a dab hand at Oxford, as I remember. Still at it? Wise
man. Sensible chap. My goodness, it's years. When did we last
meet? I have a suspicion we last dined together in '38, at the
club. Does that accord with your recollection? Croxley was
there, yes, Wyatt, it all comes back to me, Burston-Smith.

What a bunch. What a night, as I recall. All dead now, of course. No, no! I'm a fool. I'm an idiot. Our last encounter – I remember it well. Pavilion at Lord's in '39, against the West Indies, Hutton and Compton batting superbly, Constantine bowling, war looming. Surely I'm right? We shared a particularly fine bottle of port. You look as fit now as you did then. Did you have a good war?

BRIGGS *comes in with coffee, places it on table.*

Oh thank you, Denson. Leave it there, will you? That will do.

BRIGGS *leaves the room.*

How's Emily? What a woman. (*Pouring.*) Black? Here you are. What a woman. Have to tell you I fell in love with her once upon a time. Have to confess it to you. Took her out to tea, in Dorchester. Told her of my yearning. Decided to take the bull by the horns. Proposed that she betray you. Admitted you were a damn fine chap, but pointed out I would be taking nothing that belonged to you, simply that portion of herself all women keep in reserve, for a rainy day. Had an infernal job persuading her. Said she adored you, her life would be meaningless were she to be false. Plied her with buttered scones, Wiltshire cream, crumpets and strawberries. Eventually she succumbed. Don't suppose you ever knew about it, what? Oh, we're too old now for it to matter, don't you agree?

He sits, with coffee.

I rented a little cottage for the summer. She used to motor to me twice or thrice a week. I was an integral part of her shopping expeditions. You were both living on the farm then. That's right. Her father's farm. She would come to me at tea-time, or at coffee-time, the innocent hours. That summer she was mine, while you imagined her to be solely yours.

He sips the coffee.

She loved the cottage. She loved the flowers. As did I. Narcissi, crocus, dog's tooth violets, fuchsia, jonquils, pinks, verbena.

Pause

Her delicate hands.

Pause

I'll never forget her way with jonquils.

Pause

Do you remember once, was it in '37, you took her to France? I was on the same boat. Kept to my cabin. While you were doing your exercises she came to me. Her ardour was, in my experience, unparalleled. Ah well.

Pause

You were always preoccupied with your physical . . condition . . weren't you? Don't blame you. Damn fine figure of a chap. Natural athlete. Medals, scrolls, your name inscribed in gold. Once a man has breasted the tape, alone, he is breasting the tape forever. His golden moment can never be tarnished. Do you run still? Why was it we saw so little of each other, after we came down from Oxford? I mean, you had another string to your bow, did you not? You were a literary man. As was I. Yes, yes, I know we shared the occasional picnic, with Tubby Wells and all that crowd, we shared the occasional whisky and soda at the club, but we were never close, were we? I wonder why. Of course I was successful awfully early.

Pause

You did say you had a good war, didn't you?

SPOONER

A rather good one, yes.

HIRST

How splendid. The RAF?

SPOONER

The Navy.

HIRST

How splendid. Destroyers?

SPOONER

Torpedo boats.

HIRST

First rate. Kill any Germans?

SPOONER

One or two.

HIRST

Well done.

SPOONER

And you?

HIRST

I was in Military Intelligence.

SPOONER

Ah.

Pause

> HIRST

You pursued your literary career, after the war?

> SPOONER

Oh yes.

> HIRST

So did I.

> SPOONER

I believe you've done rather well.

> HIRST

Oh quite well, yes. Past my best now.

> SPOONER

Do you ever see Stella?

Pause

> HIRST

Stella?

> SPOONER

You can't have forgotten.

> HIRST

Stella who?

> SPOONER

Stella Winstanley.

HIRST

Winstanley?

SPOONER

Bunty Winstanley's sister.

HIRST

Oh, Bunty. No, I never see her.

SPOONER

You were rather taken with her.

HIRST

Was I, old chap? How did you know?

SPOONER

I was terribly fond of Bunty. He was most dreadfully annoyed with you. Wanted to punch you on the nose.

HIRST

What for?

SPOONER

For seducing his sister.

HIRST

What business was it of his?

SPOONER

He was her brother.

HIRST

That's my point.

Pause

What on earth are you driving at?

SPOONER

Bunty introduced Rupert to Stella. He was very fond of Rupert. He gave the bride away. He and Rupert were terribly old friends. He threatened to horsewhip you.

HIRST

Who did?

SPOONER

Bunty.

HIRST

He never had the guts to speak to me himself.

SPOONER

Stella begged him not to. She implored him to stay his hand. She implored him not to tell Rupert.

HIRST

I see. But who told Bunty?

SPOONER

I told Bunty. I was frightfully fond of Bunty. I was also frightfully fond of Stella.

Pause

HIRST

You appear to have been a close friend of the family.

SPOONER

Mainly of Arabella's. We used to ride together.

HIRST

Arabella Hinscott?

SPOONER

Yes.

HIRST

I knew her at Oxford.

SPOONER

So did I.

HIRST

I was very fond of Arabella.

SPOONER

Arabella was very fond of me. Bunty was never sure of precisely
how fond she was of me, nor of what form her fondness took.

HIRST

What in God's name do you mean?

SPOONER

Bunty trusted me. I was best man at their wedding. He also
trusted Arabella.

HIRST

I should warn you that I was always extremely fond of Arabella.
Her father was my tutor. I used to stay at their house.

SPOONER

I knew her father well. He took a great interest in me.

HIRST

Arabella was a girl of the most refined and organised sensi-
bilities.

SPOONER

I agree.

Pause

HIRST

Are you trying to tell me that you had an affair with Arabella?

SPOONER

A form of an affair. She had no wish for full consummation.
She was content with her particular predilection. Consuming
the male member.

HIRST *stands.*

HIRST

I'm beginning to believe you're a scoundrel. How dare you
speak of Arabella Hinscott in such a fashion? I'll have you
blackballed from the club!

SPOONER

Oh my dear sir, may I remind you that you betrayed Stella
Winstanley with Emily Spooner, my own wife, throughout a
long and soiled summer, a fact known at the time throughout
the Home Counties? May I further remind you that Muriel
Blackwood and Doreen Busby have never recovered from your
insane and corrosive sexual absolutism? May I further remind
you that your friendship with and corruption of Geoffrey
Ramsden at Oxford was the talk of Balliol and Christchurch
Cathedral?

HIRST

This is scandalous! How dare you? I'll have you horse-whipped!

SPOONER

It is you, sir, who have behaved scandalously. To the fairest of sexes, of which my wife was the fairest representative. It is you who have behaved unnaturally and scandalously, to the woman who was joined to me in God.

HIRST

I, sir? Unnaturally? Scandalously?

SPOONER

Scandalously. She told me all.

HIRST

You listen to the drivellings of a farmer's wife?

SPOONER

Since I was the farmer, yes.

HIRST

You were no farmer, sir. A weekend wanker.

SPOONER

I wrote my Homage to Wessex in the summerhouse at West Upfield.

HIRST

I have never had the good fortune to read it.

SPOONER

It is written in terza rima, a form which, if you will forgive my saying so, you have never been able to master.

HIRST

This is outrageous! Who are you? What are you doing in my house?

He goes to the door and calls.

Denson! A whisky and soda!

He walks about the room.

You are clearly a lout. The Charles Wetherby I knew was a gentleman. I see a figure reduced. I am sorry for you. Where is the moral ardour that sustained you once? Gone down the hatch.

BRIGGS *enters, pours whisky and soda, gives it to* HIRST. HIRST *looks at it.*

Down the hatch. Right down the hatch. (*He drinks.*) I do not understand . . . I do not understand . . . and I see it all about me . . . continually . . . how the most sensitive and cultivated of men can so easily change, almost overnight, into the bully, the cutpurse, the brigand. In my day nobody changed. A man was. Only religion could alter him, and that at least was a glorious misery.

He drinks, and sits in his chair.

We are not banditti here. I am prepared to be patient. I shall be kind to you. I shall show you my library. I might even show you my study. I might even show you my pen, and my blottingpad. I might even show you my footstool.

He holds out his glass.

Another.

BRIGGS *takes glass, fills it, returns it.*

I might even show you my photograph album. You might even
see a face in it which might remind you of your own, of what
you once were. You might see faces of others, in shadow, or
cheeks of others, turning, or jaws, or backs of necks, or eyes,
dark under hats, which might remind you of others, whom
once you knew, whom you thought long dead, but from whom
you will still receive a sidelong glance, if you can face the good
ghost. Allow the love of the good ghost. They possess all that
emotion . . . trapped. Bow to it. It will assuredly never release
them, but who knows . . . what relief . . . it may give to
them . . . who knows how they may quicken . . . in their chains,
in their glass jars. You think it cruel . . . to quicken them, when
they are fixed, imprisoned? No . . no. Deeply, deeply, they
wish to respond to your touch, to your look, and when you
smile, their joy . . . is unbounded. And so I say to you, tender
the dead, as you would yourself be tendered, now, in what you
would describe as your life.

He drinks.

BRIGGS
They're blank, mate, blank. The blank dead.

Silence

HIRST
Nonsense.

Pause

Pass the bottle.

                              BRIGGS
No.

                              HIRST
What?

                              BRIGGS
I said no.

                              HIRST
No pranks. No mischief. Give me the bottle.

Pause

                              BRIGGS
I've refused.

                              HIRST
Refusal can lead to dismissal.

                              BRIGGS
You can't dismiss me.

                              HIRST
Why not?

                              BRIGGS
Because I won't go.

                              HIRST
If I tell you to go, you will go. Give me the bottle.

Silence

HIRST *turns to* SPOONER.

HIRST

Bring me the bottle.

SPOONER *goes to cabinet.* BRIGGS *does not move.*
SPOONER *picks up whisky bottle, takes it to* HIRST.
HIRST *pours and places bottle at his side.*

BRIGGS

I'll have one myself.

BRIGGS *takes a glass to the bottle, pours and drinks.*

HIRST

What impertinence. Well, it doesn't matter. He was always a
scallywag. Is it raining? It so often rains, in August, in England.
Do you ever examine the gullies of the English countryside?
Under the twigs, under the dead leaves, you'll find tennis balls,
blackened. Girls threw them for their dogs, or children, for
each other, they rolled into the gully. They are lost there, given
up for dead, centuries old.

FOSTER *comes into the room.*

FOSTER

It's time for your morning walk.

Pause

I said it's time for your morning walk.

HIRST

My morning walk? No, no, I'm afraid I don't have the time
this morning.

FOSTER

It's time for your walk across the Heath.

HIRST

I can't possibly. I'm too busy. I have too many things to do.

FOSTER

What's that you're drinking?

SPOONER

The great malt which wounds.

HIRST

(*To* SPOONER.) My God, you haven't got a drink. Where's your glass?

SPOONER

Thank you. It would be unwise to mix my drinks.

HIRST

Mix?

SPOONER

I was drinking champagne.

HIRST

Of course you were, of course. Albert, another bottle.

BRIGGS

Certainly, sir.

BRIGGS *goes out.*

HIRST

I can't possibly. I have too many things to do. I have an essay to write. A critical essay. We'll have to check the files, find out what it is I'm supposed to be appraising. At the moment it's slipped my mind.

SPOONER

I could help you there.

HIRST

Oh?

SPOONER

On two counts. Firstly, I have the nose of a ferret. I can find anything in a file. Secondly, I have written any number of critical essays myself. Do you actually have a secretary?

FOSTER

I'm his secretary.

SPOONER

A secretarial post does less than justice to your talents. A young poet should travel. Travel and suffer. Join the navy, perhaps, and see the sea. Voyage and explore.

FOSTER

I've sailored. I've been there and back. I'm here where I'm needed.

BRIGGS *enters with champagne, stops at door, listens.*

SPOONER

(*To* HIRST.) You mentioned a photograph album. I could go through it with you. I could put names to the faces. A proper

exhumation could take place. Yes, I am confident that I could
be of enormous aid in that area.

FOSTER

Those faces are nameless, friend.

BRIGGS *comes into room, sets down champagne bucket.*

BRIGGS

And they'll always be nameless.

HIRST

There are places in my heart . . . where no living soul . . . has
. . . or can ever . . . trespass.

BRIGGS *opens champagne, pours glass for* SPOONER.

BRIGGS

Here you are. Fresh as a daisy. (*To* HIRST.) A drop for you,
sir?

HIRST

No, no. I'll stay . . . where I am.

BRIGGS

I'll join Mr. Friend, if I may, sir?

HIRST

Naturally.

BRIGGS

(*To* FOSTER.) Where's your glass?

FOSTER

No thanks.

HIRST

Oh come on, be sociable. Be sociable. Consort with the society to which you're attached. To which you're attached as if by bonds of steel. Mingle.

BRIGGS *pours a glass for* FOSTER.

FOSTER

It isn't even lunchtime.

BRIGGS

The best time to drink champagne is before lunch, you cunt.

FOSTER

Don't call me a cunt.

HIRST

We three, never forget, are the oldest of friends.

BRIGGS

That's why I called him a cunt.

FOSTER

(*To* BRIGGS.) Stop talking.

HIRST *lifts his glass.*

HIRST

To our good fortune.

Mutters of 'Cheers'. *They all drink.*
HIRST *looks at the window.*

HIRST

The light . . . out there . . . is gloomy . . . hardly daylight at all.
It is falling, rapidly. Distasteful. Let us close the curtains. Put
the lamps on.

BRIGGS *closes the curtains, lights lamps.*

HIRST

Ah. What relief.

Pause

How happy it is.

Pause

Today I shall come to a conclusion. There are certain matters
. . . which today I shall resolve.

SPOONER

I'll help you.

FOSTER

I was in Bali when they sent for me. I didn't have to leave, I
didn't have to come here. But I felt I was . . . called . . . I had
no alternative. I didn't have to leave that beautiful isle. But I
was intrigued. I was only a boy. But I was nondescript and
anonymous. A famous writer wanted me. He wanted me to be
his secretary, his chauffeur, his housekeeper, his amanuensis.
How did he know of me? Who told him?

SPOONER

He made an imaginative leap. Few can do it. Few do it. He did
it. And that's why God loves him.

BRIGGS

You came on my recommendation. I've always liked youth because you can use it. But it has to be open and honest. If it isn't open and honest you can't use it. I recommended you. You were open, the whole world before you.

FOSTER

I find the work fruitful. I'm in touch with a very special intelligence. This intelligence I find nourishing. I have been nourished by it. It's enlarged me. Therefore it's an intelligence worth serving. I find its demands natural. Not only that. They're legal. I'm not doing anything crooked. It's a relief. I could so easily have been bent. I have a sense of dignity in my work, a sense of honour. It never leaves me. Of service to a cause.

He refers to BRIGGS.

He is my associate. He was my proposer. I've learnt a great deal from him. He's been my guide. The most unselfish person I've ever met. He'll tell you. Let him speak.

BRIGGS

Who to?

FOSTER

What?

BRIGGS

Speak? Who to?

FOSTER *looks at* SPOONER.

FOSTER

To . . . him.

BRIGGS

To him? To a pisshole collector? To a shithouse operator? To a jamrag vendor? What the fuck are you talking about? Look at him. He's a mingejuice bottler, a fucking shitcake baker. What are you talking to him for?

HIRST

Yes, yes, but he's a good man at heart. I knew him at Oxford.

Silence

SPOONER

(*To* HIRST.) Let me live with you and be your secretary.

HIRST

Is there a big fly in here? I hear buzzing.

SPOONER

No.

HIRST

You say no.

SPOONER

Yes.

Pause

I ask you . . . to consider me for the post. If I were wearing a suit such as your own you would see me in a different light. I'm extremely good with tradespeople, hawkers, canvassers, nuns. I can be silent when desired or, when desired, convivial. I can discuss any subject of your choice – the future of the country, wild flowers, the Olympic Games. It is true I have fallen on hard times, but my imagination and intelligence are unimpaired. My will to work has not been eroded. I remain capable of undertaking the gravest and most daunting responsibilities. Temperamentally I can be what you wish. My character is, at core, a humble one. I am an honest man and, moreover, I am not too old to learn. My cooking is not to be sneezed at. I lean towards French cuisine but food without frills is not beyond my competency. I have a keen eye for dust. My kitchen would be immaculate. I am tender towards objects. I would take good care of your silver. I play chess, billiards, and the piano. I could play Chopin for you. I could read the Bible to you. I am a good companion.

Pause

My career, I admit it freely, has been chequered. I was one of the golden of my generation. Something happened. I don't know what it was. Nevertheless I am I and have survived insult and deprivation. I am I. I offer myself not abjectly but with ancient pride. I come to you as a warrior. I shall be happy to serve you as my master. I bend my knee to your excellence. I am furnished with the qualities of piety, prudence, liberality and goodness. Decline them at your peril. It is my task as a gentleman to remain amiable in my behaviour, courageous in my undertakings, discreet and gallant in my executions, by which I mean your private life would remain your own. However, I shall be sensible to the least wrong offered you. My sword shall be ready to dissever all manifest embodiments of malign forces that conspire to your ruin. I shall regard it as incumbent upon me to preserve a clear countenance and a clean conscience. I will accept death's challenge on your behalf. I shall meet it, for your sake, boldly, whether it be in the field or in the bedchamber. I am your Chevalier. I had rather bury myself in a tomb of honour than permit your dignity to be sullied by domestic enemy or foreign foe. I am yours to command.

Silence

HIRST *is still, sitting.*
FOSTER *and* BRIGGS *are still, standing.*

SPOONER

Before you reply, I would like to say one thing more. I
occasionally organise poetry readings, in the upstairs room of a
particular public house. They are reasonably well attended,
mainly by the young. I would be happy to offer you an evening
of your own. You could read your own work, to an interested
and informed audience, to an audience brimming over with
potential for the greatest possible enthusiasm. I can guarantee
a full house, and I will be happy to arrange a straightforward
fee for you or, if you prefer, a substantial share of the profits.
The young, I can assure you, would flock to hear you. My committee would deem it a singular honour to act as your host.
You would be introduced by an authority on your work, perhaps myself. After the reading, which I am confident will be a
remarkable success, we could repair to the bar below, where the
landlord – who happens to be a friend of mine – would I know
be overjoyed to entertain you, with the compliments of the
house. Nearby is an Indian restaurant of excellent standing, at
which you would be the guest of my committee. Your face is so
seldom seen, your words, known to so many, have been so
seldom heard, in the absolute authority of your own rendering,
that this event would qualify for that rarest of categories: the
unique. I beg you to consider seriously the social implications
of such an adventure. You would be there in body. It would
bring you to the young, the young to you. The elderly, also,
those who have almost lost hope, would on this occasion leave
their homes and present themselves. You would have no
trouble with the press. I would take upon myself the charge of

keeping them from nuisance. Perhaps you might agree to half a dozen photographs or so, but no more. Unless of course you positively wished, on such an occasion, to speak. Unless you preferred to hold, let us say, a small press conference, after the reading, before supper, whereby you could speak through the press to the world. But that is by the by, and would in no sense be a condition. Let us content ourselves with the idea of an intimate reading, in a pleasing and conducive environment, let us consider an evening to be remembered, by all who take part in her.

Silence

HIRST

Let us change the subject.

Pause

For the last time.

Pause

What have I said?

FOSTER

You said you're changing the subject for the last time.

HIRST

But what does that mean?

FOSTER

It means you'll never change the subject again.

HIRST

Never?

FOSTER

Never.

HIRST

Never?

FOSTER

You said for the last time.

HIRST

But what does that *mean*? What does it *mean*?

FOSTER

It means forever. It means that the subject is changed once and
for all and for the last time forever. If the subject is winter, for
instance, it'll be winter forever.

HIRST

Is the subject winter?

FOSTER

The subject is now winter. So it'll therefore be winter forever

BRIGGS

And for the last time.

FOSTER

Which will last forever. If the subject is winter, for example
spring will never come.

HIRST

But let me ask you – I must ask you –

FOSTER

Summer will never come.

BRIGGS

The trees –

FOSTER

Will never bud.

HIRST

I must ask you –

BRIGGS

Snow –

FOSTER

Will fall forever. Because you've changed the subject. For the last time.

HIRST

But have we? That's my question. Have I? Have we changed the subject?

FOSTER

Of course. The previous subject is closed.

HIRST

What was the previous subject?

FOSTER

It's forgotten. You've changed it.

HIRST

What is the present subject?

FOSTER

That there is no possibility of changing the subject since the subject has now been changed.

BRIGGS

For the last time.

FOSTER

So that nothing else will happen forever. You'll simply be sitting here forever.

BRIGGS

But not alone.

FOSTER

No. We'll be with you. Briggs and me.

Pause

HIRST

It's night.

FOSTER

And will always be night.

BRIGGS

Because the subject –

FOSTER

Can never be changed.

Silence

HIRST

But I hear sounds of birds. Don't you hear them? Sounds I never heard before. I hear them as they must have sounded

hen, when I was young, although I never heard them then,
lthough they sounded about us then.

Pause

Yes. It is true. I am walking towards a lake. Someone is
ollowing me, through the trees. I lose him, easily. I see a body
n the water, floating. I am excited. I look closer and see I was
mistaken. There is nothing in the water. I say to myself, I saw a
body, drowning. But I am mistaken. There is nothing there.

Silence

SPOONER

No. You are in no man's land. Which never moves, which never
changes, which never grows older, but which remains forever,
icy and silent.

Silence

HIRST

'll drink to that.

He drinks.

SLOW FADE

Betrayal

Betrayal was first presented by the National Theatre, London, on 15th November 1978 with the following cast:

EMMA	Penelope Wilton
JERRY	Michael Gambon
ROBERT	Daniel Massey
A WAITER	Artro Morris

Designed by John Bury
Directed by Peter Hall

In 1977 Emma is 38, Jerry and Robert are 40.

Betrayal can be performed without an interval, or with an interval after Scene Four.

H.P.

1977

Scene One

Pub. 1977. Spring.

Noon.

EMMA is sitting at a corner table. JERRY approaches with drinks, a pint of bitter for him, a glass of wine for her.

He sits. They smile, toast each other silently, drink.

He sits back and looks at her.

                    JERRY
Well . . .

                    EMMA
How are you?

                    JERRY
All right.

                    EMMA
You look well.

                    JERRY
Well, I'm not all that well, really.

                    EMMA
Why? What's the matter?

JERRY

Hangover.

He raises his glass.

Cheers.

He drinks.

How are you?

EMMA

I'm fine.

She looks round the bar, back at him.

Just like old times.

JERRY

Mmn. It's been a long time.

EMMA

Yes.

Pause

I thought of you the other day.

JERRY

Good God. Why?

She laughs.

JERRY

Why?

EMMA

Well, it's nice, sometimes, to think back. Isn't it?

JERRY

Absolutely.

Pause

How's everything?

EMMA

Oh, not too bad.

Pause

Do you know how long it is since we met?

JERRY

Well I came to that private view, when was it – ?

EMMA

No, I don't mean that.

JERRY

Oh you mean alone?

EMMA

Yes.

JERRY

Uuh . . .

EMMA

Two years.

JERRY

Yes, I thought it must be. Mmnn.

Pause

EMMA

Long time.

JERRY

Yes. It is.

Pause

How's it going? The Gallery?

EMMA

How do you think it's going?

JERRY

Well. Very well, I would say.

EMMA

I'm glad you think so. Well, it is, actually. I enjoy it.

JERRY

Funny lot, painters, aren't they?

EMMA

They're not at all funny.

JERRY

Aren't they? What a pity.

Pause

How's Robert?

EMMA

When did you last see him?

JERRY

I haven't seen him for months. Don't know why. Why?

EMMA

Why what?

JERRY

Why did you ask when I last saw him?

EMMA

I just wondered. How's Sam?

JERRY

You mean Judith.

EMMA

Do I?

JERRY

You remember the form. I ask about your husband, you ask about my wife.

EMMA

Yes, of course. How is your wife?

JERRY

All right.

Pause

EMMA

Sam must be ... tall.

JERRY

He is tall. Quite tall. Does a lot of running. He's a long distance runner. He wants to be a zoologist.

EMMA

No, really? Good. And Sarah?

JERRY

She's ten.

EMMA

God. I suppose she must be.

JERRY

Yes, she must be.

Pause

Ned's five, isn't he?

EMMA

You remember.

JERRY

Well, I would remember that.

Pause

EMMA

Yes.

Pause

You're all right, though?

JERRY

Oh ... yes, sure.

Pause

EMMA

Ever think of me?

JERRY

I don't need to think of you.

EMMA

Oh?

JERRY

I don't need to *think* of you.

Pause

Anyway I'm all right. How are you?

EMMA

Fine, really. All right.

JERRY

You're looking very pretty.

EMMA

Really? Thank you. I'm glad to see you.

JERRY

So am I. I mean to see you.

EMMA

You think of me sometimes?

JERRY

I think of you sometimes.

Pause

I saw Charlotte the other day.

EMMA

No? Where? She didn't mention it.

JERRY

She didn't see me. In the street.

EMMA

But you haven't seen her for years.

JERRY

I recognised her.

EMMA

How could you? How could you know?

JERRY

I did.

EMMA

What did she look like?

JERRY

You.

EMMA

No, what did you think of her, really?

JERRY

I thought she was lovely.

EMMA

Yes. She's very ... She's smashing. She's thirteen.

Pause

Do you remember that time ... oh god it was ... when you
picked her up and threw her up and caught her?

JERRY

She was very light.

EMMA

She remembers that, you know.

JERRY

Really?

EMMA

Mmnn. Being thrown up.

JERRY

What a memory.

Pause

She doesn't know ... about us, does she?

EMMA

Of course not. She just remembers you, as an old friend.

JERRY

That's right.

Pause

Yes, everyone was there that day, standing around, your husband, my wife, all the kids, I remember.

EMMA

What day?

JERRY

When I threw her up. It was in your kitchen.

EMMA

It was in your kitchen.

Silence

JERRY

Darling.

EMMA

Don't say that.

Pause

It all . . .

JERRY

Seems such a long time ago.

EMMA

Does it?

JERRY

Same again?

He takes the glasses, goes to the bar. She sits still. He returns, with the drinks, sits.

EMMA

I thought of you the other day.

Pause

I was driving through Kilburn. Suddenly I saw where I was. I just stopped, and then I turned down Kinsale Drive and drove into Wessex Grove. I drove past the house and then stopped about fifty yards further on, like we used to do, do you remember?

JERRY

Yes.

EMMA

People were coming out of the house. They walked up the road.

JERRY

What sort of people?

EMMA

Oh . . . young people. Then I got out of the car and went up the steps. I looked at the bells, you know, the names on the bells. I looked for our name.

Pause

JERRY

Green.

Pause

Couldn't see it, eh?

EMMA

No.

JERRY

That's because we're not there any more. We haven't been there for years.

EMMA

No we haven't.

Pause

JERRY

I hear you're seeing a bit of Casey.

EMMA

What?

JERRY

Casey. I just heard you were . . . seeing a bit of him.

EMMA

Where did you hear that?

JERRY

Oh . . . people . . . talking.

EMMA

Christ.

JERRY

The funny thing was that the only thing I really felt was irritation, I mean irritation that nobody gossiped about us like that, in the old days. I nearly said, now look, she may be having the occasional drink with Casey, who cares, but she and I had an affair for seven years and none of you bastards had the faintest idea it was happening.

Pause

EMMA

I wonder. I wonder if everyone knew, all the time.

JERRY

Don't be silly. We were brilliant. Nobody knew. Who ever went to Kilburn in those days? Just you and me.

Pause

Anyway, what's all this about you and Casey?

EMMA

What do you mean?

JERRY

What's going on?

EMMA

We have the occasional drink.

JERRY

I thought you didn't admire his work.

EMMA

I've changed. Or his work has changed. Are you jealous?

JERRY

Of what?

Pause

I couldn't be jealous of Casey. I'm his agent. I advised him about his divorce. I read all his first drafts. I persuaded your husband to publish his first novel. I escort him to Oxford to speak at the Union. He's my . . . he's my boy. I discovered him when he was a poet, and that's a bloody long time ago now.

Pause

He's even taken me down to Southampton to meet his Mum and Dad. I couldn't be jealous of Casey. Anyway it's not as if we're having an affair now, is it? We haven't seen each other for years. Really, I'm very happy if you're happy.

Pause

What about Robert?

Pause

EMMA

Well ... I think we're going to separate.

JERRY

Oh?

EMMA

We had a long talk ... last night.

JERRY

Last night?

EMMA

You know what I found out ... last night? He's betrayed me
for years. He's had ... other women for years.

JERRY

No? Good Lord.

Pause

But we betrayed him for years.

EMMA

And he betrayed me for years.

JERRY

Well I never knew that.

EMMA

Nor did I.

Pause

JERRY

Does Casey know about this?

EMMA

I wish you wouldn't keep calling him Casey. His name is Roger.

JERRY

Yes. Roger.

EMMA

I phoned *you*. I don't know why.

JERRY

What a funny thing. We were such close friends, weren't we? Robert and me, even though I haven't seen him for a few months, but through all those years, all the drinks, all the lunches . . . we had together, I never even gleaned . . . I never suspected . . . that there was anyone else . . . in his life but you. Never. For example, when you're with a fellow in a pub, or a restaurant, for example, from time to time he pops out for a piss, you see, who doesn't, but what I mean is, if he's making a crafty telephone call, you can sort of sense it, you see, you can sense the pip pip pips. Well, I never did that with Robert. He never made any pip pip telephone calls in any pub I was ever with him in. The funny thing is that it was me who made the pip pip calls – to you, when I left him boozing at the bar. That's the funny thing.

Pause

When did he tell you all this?

EMMA

Last night. I think we were up all night.

Pause

JERRY

You talked all night?

EMMA

Yes. Oh yes.

Pause

JERRY

I didn't come into it, did I?

EMMA

What?

JERRY

I just –

EMMA

I just phoned you this morning, you know, that's all, because
I . . . because we're old friends . . . I've been up all night . . .
the whole thing's finished . . . I suddenly felt I wanted to see
you.

JERRY

Well, look, I'm happy to see you. I am. I'm sorry ...
about ...

EMMA

Do you remember? I mean, you do remember?

JERRY

I remember.

Pause

EMMA

You couldn't really afford Wessex Grove when we took it,
could you?

JERRY

Oh, love finds a way.

EMMA

I bought the curtains.

JERRY

You found a way.

EMMA

Listen, I didn't want to see you for nostalgia, I mean what's
the point? I just wanted to see how you were. Truly. How are
you?

JERRY

Oh what does it matter?

Pause

You didn't tell Robert about me last night, did you?

EMMA

I had to.

Pause

He told me everything. I told him everything. We were up
. . . all night. At one point Ned came down. I had to take him
up to bed, had to put him back to bed. Then I went down
again. I think it was the voices woke him up. You know . . .

JERRY

You told him everything?

EMMA

I had to.

JERRY

You told him everything . . . about us?

EMMA

I had to.

Pause

JERRY

But he's my oldest friend. I mean, I picked his own daughter
up in my own arms and threw her up and caught her, in my
kitchen. He watched me do it.

EMMA

It doesn't matter. It's all gone.

JERRY

Is it? What has?

EMMA

It's all all over.

She drinks.

1977 Later

Scene Two

Jerry's House. Study. 1977. Spring.

JERRY *sitting*. ROBERT *standing, with glass*.

JERRY
It's good of you to come.

ROBERT
Not at all.

JERRY
Yes, yes, I know it was difficult ... I know ... the kids ...

ROBERT
It's all right. It sounded urgent.

JERRY
Well ... You found someone, did you?

ROBERT
What?

JERRY
For the kids.

ROBERT

Yes, yes. Honestly. Everything's in order. Anyway, Charlotte's not a baby.

JERRY

No.

Pause

Are you going to sit down?

ROBERT

Well, I might, yes, in a minute.

Pause

JERRY

Judith's at the hospital . . . on night duty. The kids are . . . here . . . upstairs.

ROBERT

Uh – huh.

JERRY

I must speak to you. It's important.

ROBERT

Speak.

JERRY

Yes.

Pause

ROBERT

You look quite rough.

Pause

What's the trouble?

Pause

It's not about you and Emma, is it?

Pause

I know all about that.

JERRY

Yes. So I've ... been told.

ROBERT

Ah.

Pause

Well, it's not very important, is it? Been over for years, hasn't it?

JERRY

It is important.

ROBERT

Really? Why?

JERRY *stands, walks about.*

JERRY

I thought I was going to go mad.

ROBERT

When?

JERRY

This evening. Just now. Wondering whether to phone you. I
had to phone you. It took me . . . two hours to phone you.
And then you were with the kids . . . I thought I wasn't going
to be able to see you . . . I thought I'd go mad. I'm very
grateful to you . . . for coming.

ROBERT

Oh for God's sake! Look, what exactly do you want to say?

Pause

JERRY *sits*.

JERRY

I don't know why she told you. I don't know how she could
tell you. I just don't understand. Listen, I know you've got
. . . look, I saw her today . . . we had a drink . . . I haven't seen
her for . . . she told me, you know, that you're in trouble,
both of you . . . and so on. I know that. I mean I'm sorry.

ROBERT

Don't be sorry.

JERRY

Why not?

Pause

The fact is I can't understand . . . why she thought it necessary . . . after all these years . . . to tell you . . . so suddenly . . . last night . . .

ROBERT

Last night?

JERRY

Without consulting me. Without even warning me. After all, you and me . . .

ROBERT

She didn't tell me last night.

JERRY

What do you mean?

Pause

I know about last night. She told me about it. You were up all night, weren't you?

ROBERT

That's correct.

JERRY

And she told you . . . last night . . . about her and me. Did she not?

ROBERT

No, she didn't. She didn't tell me about you and her last night. She told me about you and her four years ago.

Pause

So she didn't have to tell me again last night. Because I knew. And she knew I knew because she told me herself four years ago.

Silence

JERRY

What?

ROBERT

I think I will sit down.

He sits.

I thought you knew.

JERRY

Knew what?

ROBERT

That I knew. That I've known for years. I thought you knew that.

JERRY

You thought I knew?

ROBERT

She said you didn't. But I didn't believe that.

Pause

Anyway I think I thought you knew. But you say you didn't?

JERRY

She told you . . . when?

ROBERT

Well, I found out. That's what happened. I told her I'd found
out and then she . . . confirmed . . . the facts.

JERRY

When?

ROBERT

Oh, a long time ago, Jerry.

Pause

JERRY

But we've seen each other . . . a great deal . . . over the last
four years. We've had lunch.

ROBERT

Never played squash though.

JERRY

I was your best friend.

ROBERT

Well, yes, sure.

JERRY *stares at him and then holds his head in his hands.*

Oh, don't get upset. There's no point.

Silence

JERRY *sits up.*

                    JERRY

Why didn't she tell me?

                    ROBERT

Well, I'm not her, old boy.

                    JERRY

Why didn't you tell me?

Pause

                    ROBERT

I thought you might know.

                    JERRY

But you didn't know for *certain*, did you? You didn't *know*!

                    ROBERT

No.

                    JERRY

Then why didn't you tell me?

Pause

                    ROBERT

Tell you what?

                    JERRY

That you knew. You bastard.

ROBERT

Oh, don't call me a bastard, Jerry.

Pause

JERRY

What are we going to do?

ROBERT

You and I are not going to do anything. My marriage is
finished. I've just got to make proper arrangements, that's
all. About the children.

Pause

JERRY

You hadn't thought of telling Judith?

ROBERT

Telling Judith what? Oh, about you and Emma. You mean
she never knew? Are you quite sure?

Pause

No, I hadn't thought of telling Judith, actually. You don't
seem to understand. You don't seem to understand that I
don't give a shit about any of this. It's true I've hit Emma
once or twice. But that wasn't to defend a principle. I wasn't
inspired to do it from any kind of moral standpoint. I just felt
like giving her a good bashing. The old itch . . . you understand.

Pause

JERRY

But you betrayed her for years, didn't you?

ROBERT

Oh yes.

JERRY

And she never knew about it. Did she?

ROBERT

Didn't she?

Pause

JERRY

I didn't.

ROBERT

No, you didn't know very much about anything, really, did you?

Pause

JERRY

No.

ROBERT

Yes you did.

JERRY

Yes I did. I lived with her.

ROBERT

Yes. In the afternoons.

JERRY

Sometimes very long ones. For seven years.

ROBERT

Yes, you certainly knew all there was to know about that. About the seven years of afternoons. I don't know anything about that.

Pause

I hope she looked after you all right.

Silence

JERRY

We used to like each other.

ROBERT

We still do.

Pause

I bumped into old Casey the other day. I believe he's having an affair with my wife. We haven't played squash for years, Casey and me. We used to have a damn good game.

JERRY

He's put on weight.

ROBERT

Yes, I thought that.

JERRY

He's over the hill.

ROBERT

Is he?

JERRY

Don't you think so?

ROBERT

In what respect?

JERRY

His work. His books.

ROBERT

Oh his books. His art. Yes his art does seem to be falling away, doesn't it?

JERRY

Still sells.

ROBERT

Oh, sells very well. Sells very well indeed. Very good for us. For you and me.

JERRY

Yes.

ROBERT

Someone was telling me – who was it – must have been someone in the publicity department – the other day – that when Casey went up to York to sign his latest book, in a bookshop, you know, with Barbara Spring, you know, the populace queued for hours to get his signature on his book, while one old lady and a dog queued to get Barbara Spring's signature, on her book. I happen to think that Barbara Spring . . . is good, don't you?

JERRY

Yes.

Pause

ROBERT

Still, we both do very well out of Casey, don't we?

JERRY

Very well.

Pause

ROBERT

Have you read any good books lately?

JERRY

I've been reading Yeats.

ROBERT

Ah. Yeats. Yes.

Pause

JERRY

You read Yeats on Torcello once.

ROBERT

On Torcello?

JERRY

Don't you remember? Years ago. You went over to Torcello in the dawn, alone. And read Yeats.

ROBERT

So I did. I told you that, yes.

Pause

Yes.

Pause

Where are you going this summer, you and the family?

JERRY

The Lake District.

1975

Scene Three

Flat. 1975. Winter

JERRY *and* EMMA. *They are sitting.*

Silence

JERRY
What do you want to do then?

Pause

EMMA
I don't quite know what we're doing, any more, that's all.

JERRY
Mmnn.

Pause

EMMA
I mean, this flat ...

JERRY
Yes.

EMMA
Can you actually remember when we were last here?

JERRY

In the summer, was it?

EMMA

Well, was it?

JERRY

I know it seems –

EMMA

It was the beginning of September.

JERRY

Well, that's summer, isn't it?

EMMA

It was actually extremely cold. It was early autumn.

JERRY

It's pretty cold now.

EMMA

We were going to get another electric fire.

JERRY

Yes, I never got that.

EMMA

Not much point in getting it if we're never here.

JERRY

We're here now.

EMMA

Not really.

Silence

JERRY

Well, things have changed. You've been so busy, your job,
and everything.

EMMA

Well, I know. But I mean, I like it. I want to do it.

JERRY

No, it's great. It's marvellous for you. But you're not –

EMMA

If you're running a gallery you've got to run it, you've got to
be there.

JERRY

But you're not free in the afternoons. Are you?

EMMA

No.

JERRY

So how can we meet?

EMMA

But look at the times you're out of the country. You're never
here.

JERRY

But when I am here you're not free in the afternoons. So we
can never meet.

EMMA

We can meet for lunch.

JERRY

We can meet for lunch but we can't come all the way out here for a quick lunch. I'm too old for that.

EMMA

I didn't suggest that.

Pause

You see, in the past . . . we were inventive, we were determined, it was . . . it seemed impossible to meet . . . impossible . . . and yet we did. We met here, we took this flat and we met in this flat because we wanted to.

JERRY

It would not matter how much we wanted to if you're not free in the afternoons and I'm in America.

Silence

Nights have always been out of the question and you know it. I have a family.

EMMA

I have a family too.

JERRY

I know that perfectly well. I might remind you that your husband is my oldest friend.

EMMA

What do you mean by that?

JERRY

I don't *mean* anything by it.

EMMA

But what are you trying to say by saying that?

JERRY

Jesus. I'm not *trying* to say anything. I've said precisely what I wanted to say.

EMMA

I see.

Pause

The fact is that in the old days we used our imagination and we'd take a night and make an arrangement and go to an hotel.

JERRY

Yes. We did.

Pause

But that was . . . in the main . . . before we got this flat.

EMMA

We haven't spent many nights . . . in this flat.

JERRY

No.

Pause

Not many nights anywhere, really.

Silence

EMMA

Can you afford ... to keep it going, month after month?

JERRY

Oh ...

EMMA

It's a waste. Nobody comes here. I just can't bear to think about it, actually. Just ... empty. All day and night. Day after day and night after night. I mean the crockery and the curtains and the bedspread and everything. And the table-cloth I brought from Venice. (*Laughs.*) It's ridiculous.

Pause

It's just ... an empty home.

JERRY

It's not a home.

Pause

I know ... I know what you wanted ... but it could never ... actually be a home. You have a home. I have a home. With curtains, etcetera. And children. Two children in two homes. There are no children here, so it's not the same kind of home.

EMMA

It was never intended to be the same kind of home. Was it?

Pause

You didn't ever see it as a home, in any sense, did you?

JERRY

No, I saw it as a flat ... you know.

EMMA

For fucking.

JERRY

No, for loving.

EMMA

Well, there's not much of that left, is there?

Silence

JERRY

I don't think we don't love each other.

Pause

EMMA

Ah well.

Pause

What will you do about all the ... furniture?

JERRY

What?

EMMA

The contents.

Silence

JERRY

You know we can do something very simple, if we want to do
it.

EMMA

You mean sell it to Mrs Banks for a small sum and . . . and she
can let it as a furnished flat?

JERRY

That's right. Wasn't the bed here?

EMMA

What?

JERRY

Wasn't it?

EMMA

We bought the bed. We bought everything. We bought the
bed together.

JERRY

Ah. Yes.

EMMA *stands*.

EMMA

You'll make all the arrangements, then? With Mrs Banks?

Pause

I don't want anything. Nowhere I can put it, you see. I have a home, with tablecloths and all the rest of it.

JERRY

I'll go into it, with Mrs Banks. There'll be a few quid, you know, so . . .

EMMA

No, I don't want any *cash*, thank you very much.

Silence. She puts coat on.

I'm going now.

He turns, looks at her.

Oh here's my key.

Takes out keyring, tries to take key from ring.

Oh Christ.

Struggles to take key from ring.
Throws him the ring.

You take it off.

He catches it, looks at her.

Can you just do it please? I'm picking up Charlotte from school. I'm taking her shopping.

He takes key off.

Do you realise this is an afternoon? It's the Gallery's afternoon off. That's why I'm here. We close every Thursday afternoon. Can I have my keyring?

He gives it to her.

Thanks. Listen. I think we've made absolutely the right decision.

She goes.

He stands.

1974

Scene Four

Robert and Emma's House. Living room. 1974. Autumn.

ROBERT *pouring a drink for* JERRY. *He goes to the door.*

ROBERT

Emma! Jerry's here!

EMMA (off)

Who?

ROBERT

Jerry.

EMMA

I'll be down.

ROBERT *gives the drink to* JERRY.

JERRY

Cheers.

ROBERT

Cheers. She's just putting Ned to bed. I should think he'll be off in a minute.

JERRY

Off where?

ROBERT

Dreamland.

JERRY

Ah. Yes, how is your sleep these days?

ROBERT

What?

JERRY

Do you still have bad nights? With Ned, I mean?

ROBERT

Oh, I see. Well, no. No, it's getting better. But you know what they say?

JERRY

What?

ROBERT

They say boys are worse than girls.

JERRY

Worse?

ROBERT

Babies. They say boy babies cry more than girl babies.

JERRY

Do they?

ROBERT

You didn't find that to be the case?

JERRY

Uh ... yes, I think we did. Did you?

ROBERT

Yes. What do you make of it? Why do you think that is?

JERRY

Well, I suppose ... boys are more anxious.

ROBERT

Boy babies?

JERRY

Yes.

ROBERT

What the hell are they anxious about ... at their age? Do you
think?

JERRY

Well ... facing the world, I suppose, leaving the womb, all
that.

ROBERT

But what about girl babies? They leave the womb too.

JERRY

That's true. It's also true that nobody talks much about girl
babies leaving the womb. Do they?

ROBERT

I am prepared to do so.

JERRY

I see. Well, what have you got to say?

ROBERT

I was asking you a question.

JERRY

What was it?

ROBERT

Why do you assert that boy babies find leaving the womb more of a problem than girl babies?

JERRY

Have I made such an assertion?

ROBERT

You went on to make a further assertion, to the effect that boy babies are more anxious about facing the world than girl babies.

JERRY

Do you yourself believe that to be the case?

ROBERT

I do, yes.

Pause

JERRY

Why do you think it is?

ROBERT

I have no answer.

Pause

JERRY

Do you think it might have something to do with the difference between the sexes?

Pause

ROBERT

Good God, you're right. That must be it.

EMMA *comes in.*

EMMA

Hullo. Surprise.

JERRY

I was having tea with Casey.

EMMA

Where?

JERRY

Just around the corner.

EMMA

I thought he lived in ... Hampstead or somewhere.

ROBERT

You're out of date.

EMMA

Am I?

JERRY

He's left Susannah. He's living alone round the corner.

EMMA

Oh.

ROBERT

Writing a novel about a man who leaves his wife and three
children and goes to live alone on the other side of London to
write a novel about a man who leaves his wife and three
children —

EMMA

I hope it's better than the last one.

ROBERT

The last one? Ah, the last one. Wasn't that the one about the
man who lived in a big house in Hampstead with his wife and
three children and is writing a novel about — ?

JERRY (*to* EMMA)

Why didn't you like it?

EMMA

I've told you actually.

JERRY

I think it's the best thing he's written.

EMMA

It may be the best thing he's *written* but it's still blood
dishonest.

JERRY

Dishonest? In what way dishonest?

EMMA

I've told you, actually.

JERRY

Have you?

ROBERT

Yes, she has. Once when we were all having dinner, I remember, you, me, Emma and Judith, where was it, Emma gave a dissertation over the pudding about dishonesty in Casey with reference to his last novel. 'Drying Out.' It was most stimulating. Judith had to leave unfortunately in the middle of it for her night shift at the hospital. How is Judith, by the way?

JERRY

Very well.

Pause

ROBERT

When are we going to play squash?

JERRY

You're too good.

ROBERT

Not at all. I'm not good at all. I'm just fitter than you.

JERRY

But why? Why are you fitter than me?

ROBERT

Because I play squash.

JERRY

Oh, you're playing? Regularly?

ROBERT

Mmnn.

JERRY

With whom?

ROBERT

Casey, actually.

JERRY

Casey? Good Lord. What's he like?

ROBERT

He's a brutally honest squash player. No, really, we haven'
played for years. We must play. You were rather good.

JERRY

Yes, I was quite good. All right. I'll give you a ring.

ROBERT

Why don't you?

JERRY

We'll make a date.

ROBERT

Right.

JERRY

es. We must do that.

ROBERT

nd then I'll take you to lunch.

JERRY

o, no. I'll take you to lunch.

ROBERT

he man who wins buys the lunch.

EMMA

n I watch?

use

ROBERT

hat?

EMMA

hy can't I watch and then take you both to lunch?

ROBERT

ell, to be brutally honest, we wouldn't actually want a
oman around, would we, Jerry? I mean a game of squash
n't simply a game of squash, it's rather more than that. You
e, first there's the game. And then there's the shower. And
en there's the pint. And then there's lunch. After all,
u've been at it. You've had your battle. What you want is
ur pint and your lunch. You really don't want a woman
ying you lunch. You don't actually want a woman within a
le of the place, any of the places, really. You don't want her
the squash court, you don't want her in the shower, or the

pub, or the restaurant. You see, at lunch you want to tal
about squash, or cricket, or books, or even women, with you
friend, and be able to warm to your theme without fear c
improper interruption. That's what it's all about. What d
you think, Jerry?

                      JERRY

I haven't played squash for years.

Pause

                      ROBERT

Well, let's play next week.

                      JERRY

I can't next week. I'm in New York.

                      EMMA

Are you?

                      JERRY

I'm going over with one of my more celebrated writers
actually.

                      EMMA

Who?

                      JERRY

Casey. Someone wants to film that novel of his you didn'
like. We're going over to discuss it. It was a question of ther
coming over here or us going over there. Casey thought h
deserved the trip.

                      EMMA

What about you?

JERRY

What?

EMMA

Do you deserve the trip?

ROBERT

Judith going?

JERRY

No. He can't go alone. We'll have that game of squash when I get back. A week, or at the most ten days.

ROBERT

Lovely.

JERRY (*to* EMMA)

Bye. Thanks for the drink.

EMMA

Bye.

ROBERT *and* JERRY *leave.*

She remains still.

ROBERT *returns. He kisses her. She responds. She breaks away, puts her head on his shoulder, cries quietly. He holds her.*

1973

Scene Five

Hotel Room. Venice. 1973. Summer.

EMMA *on bed reading.* ROBERT *at window looking out. She looks up at him, then back at the book.*

> EMMA

It's Torcello tomorrow, isn't it?

> ROBERT

What?

> EMMA

We're going to Torcello tomorrow, aren't we?

> ROBERT

Yes. That's right.

> EMMA

That'll be lovely.

> ROBERT

Mmn.

> EMMA

I can't wait.

Pause

ROBERT

Book good?

EMMA

Mmn. Yes.

ROBERT

What is it?

EMMA

This new book. This man Spinks.

ROBERT

Oh that. Jerry was telling me about it.

EMMA

Jerry? Was he?

ROBERT

He was telling me about it at lunch last week.

EMMA

Really? Does he like it?

ROBERT

Spinks is his boy. He discovered him.

EMMA

Oh. I didn't know that.

ROBERT

Unsolicited manuscript.

Pause

You think it's good, do you?

EMMA
Yes, I do. I'm enjoying it.

ROBERT
Jerry thinks it's good too. You should have lunch with us one
day and chat about it.

EMMA
Is that absolutely necessary?

Pause

It's not as good as all that.

ROBERT
You mean it's not good enough for you to have lunch with
Jerry and me and chat about it?

EMMA
What the hell are you talking about?

ROBERT
I must read it again myself, now it's in hard covers.

EMMA
Again?

ROBERT
Jerry wanted us to publish it.

EMMA

Oh, really?

ROBERT

Well, naturally. Anyway, I turned it down.

EMMA

Why?

ROBERT

Oh . . . not much more to say on that subject, really, is there?

EMMA

What do you consider the subject to be?

ROBERT

Betrayal.

EMMA

No, it isn't.

ROBERT

Isn't it? What is it then?

EMMA

I haven't finished it yet. I'll let you know.

ROBERT

Well, do let me know.

Pause

Of course, I could be thinking of the wrong book.

Silence

By the way, I went into American Express yesterday.

She looks up.

EMMA

Oh?

ROBERT

Yes. I went to cash some travellers cheques. You get a much better rate there, you see, than you do in an hotel.

EMMA

Oh, do you?

ROBERT

Oh yes. Anyway, there was a letter there for you. They asked me if you were any relation and I said yes. So they asked me if I wanted to take it. I mean, they gave it to me. But I said no, I would leave it. Did you get it?

EMMA

Yes.

ROBERT

I suppose you popped in when you were out shopping yesterday evening?

EMMA

That's right.

ROBERT

Oh well, I'm glad you got it.

Pause

To be honest, I was amazed that they suggested I take it. It could never happen in England. But these Italians . . . so free and easy. I mean, just because my name is Downs and your name is Downs doesn't mean that we're the Mr and Mrs Downs that they, in their laughing Mediterranean way, assume we are. We could be, and in fact are vastly more likely to be, total strangers. So let's say I, whom they laughingly assume to be your husband, had taken the letter, having declared myself to be your husband but in truth being a total stranger, and opened it, and read it, out of nothing more than idle curiosity, and then thrown it in a canal, you would never have received it and would have been deprived of your legal right to open your own mail, and all this because of Venetian je m'en foutisme. I've a good mind to write to the Doge of Venice about it.

Pause

That's what stopped me taking it, by the way, and bringing it to you, the thought that I could very easily be a total stranger.

Pause

What they of course did not know, and had no way of knowing, was that I am your husband.

EMMA

Pretty inefficient bunch.

ROBERT

Only in a laughing Mediterranean way.

Pause

EMMA

It was from Jerry.

ROBERT

Yes, I recognised the handwriting.

Pause

How is he?

EMMA

Okay.

ROBERT

Good. And Judith?

EMMA

Fine.

Pause

ROBERT

What about the kids?

EMMA

I don't think he mentioned them.

ROBERT

They're probably all right, then. If they were ill or something he'd have probably mentioned it.

Pause

Any other news?

EMMA

No.

Silence

ROBERT

Are you looking forward to Torcello?

Pause

How many times have we been to Torcello? Twice. I remember how you loved it, the first time I took you there. You fell in love with it. That was about ten years ago, wasn't it? About . . . six months after we were married. Yes. Do you remember? I wonder if you'll like it as much tomorrow.

Pause

What do you think of Jerry as a letter writer?

She laughs shortly.

You're trembling. Are you cold?

EMMA

No.

ROBERT

He used to write to me at one time. Long letters about Ford Madox Ford. I used to write to him too, come to think of it. Long letters about . . . oh, W. B. Yeats, I suppose. That was the time when we were both editors of poetry magazines.

Him at Cambridge, me at Oxford. Did you know that? We were bright young men. And close friends. Well, we still are close friends. All that was long before I met you. Long before he met you. I've been trying to remember when I introduced him to you. I simply can't remember. I take it I *did* introduce him to you? Yes. But when? Can you remember?

EMMA

No.

ROBERT

You can't?

EMMA

No.

ROBERT

How odd.

Pause

He wasn't best man at our wedding, was he?

EMMA

You know he was.

ROBERT

Ah yes. Well, that's probably when I introduced him to you.

Pause

Was there any message for me, in his letter?

Pause

I mean in the line of business, to do with the world of
publishing. Has he discovered any new and original talent?
He's quite talented at uncovering talent, old Jerry.

EMMA

No message.

ROBERT

No message. Not even his love?

Silence

EMMA

We're lovers.

ROBERT

Ah. Yes. I thought it might be something like that, something along those lines.

EMMA

When?

ROBERT

What?

EMMA

When did you think?

ROBERT

Yesterday. Only yesterday. When I saw his handwriting on
the letter. Before yesterday I was quite ignorant.

EMMA

Ah.

Pause

I'm sorry.

ROBERT

Sorry?

Silence

Where does it . . . take place? Must be a bit awkward. I mean we've got two kids, he's got two kids, not to mention a wife . . .

EMMA

We have a flat.

ROBERT

Ah. I see.

Pause

Nice?

Pause

A flat. It's quite well established then, your . . . uh . . . affair?

EMMA

Yes.

ROBERT

How long?

EMMA

Some time.

ROBERT

Yes, but how long exactly?

EMMA

Five years.

ROBERT

Five years?

Pause

Ned is one year old.

Pause

Did you hear what I said?

EMMA

Yes. He's your son. Jerry was in America. For two months.

Silence

ROBERT

Did he write to you from America?

EMMA

Of course. And I wrote to him.

ROBERT

Did you tell him that Ned had been conceived?

EMMA

Not by letter.

ROBERT

But when you did tell him, was he happy to know I was to be
a father?

Pause

I've always liked Jerry. To be honest, I've always liked him
rather more than I've liked you. Maybe I should have had an
affair with him myself.

Silence

Tell me, are you looking forward to our trip to Torcello?

1973 Later

Scene Six

Flat. 1973. Summer.

EMMA and JERRY standing, kissing. She is holding a basket and a parcel.

                    EMMA
Darling.

                    JERRY
Darling.

He continues to hold her. She laughs.

                    EMMA
I must put this down.

She puts basket on table.

                    JERRY
What's in it?

                    EMMA
Lunch.

                    JERRY
What?

EMMA

Things you like.

He pours wine.

How do I look?

JERRY

Beautiful.

EMMA

Do I look well?

JERRY

You do.

He gives her wine.

EMMA (*sipping*)

Mmmnn.

JERRY

How was it?

EMMA

It was lovely.

JERRY

Did you go to Torcello?

EMMA

No.

JERRY

Why not?

EMMA

Oh, I don't know. The speedboats were on strike, or something.

JERRY

On strike?

EMMA

Yes. On the day we were going.

JERRY

Ah. What about the gondolas?

EMMA

You can't take a gondola to Torcello.

JERRY

Well, they used to in the old days, didn't they? Before they had speedboats. How do you think they got over there?

EMMA

It would take hours.

JERRY

Yes, I suppose so.

Pause

I got your letter.

EMMA

Good.

JERRY

Get mine?

EMMA

Of course. Miss me?

JERRY

Yes. Actually, I haven't been well.

EMMA

What?

JERRY

Oh nothing. A bug.

She kisses him.

EMMA

I missed you.

She turns away, looks about.

You haven't been here . . . at all?

JERRY

No.

EMMA

Needs Hoovering.

JERRY

Later.

Pause

I spoke to Robert this morning.

EMMA

Oh?

JERRY

I'm taking him to lunch on Thursday.

EMMA

Thursday? Why?

JERRY

Well, it's my turn.

EMMA

No, I meant why are you taking him to lunch?

JERRY

Because it's my turn. Last time he took me to lunch.

EMMA

You know what I mean.

JERRY

No. What?

EMMA

What is the subject or point of your lunch?

JERRY

No subject or point. We've just been doing it for years. His turn, followed by my turn.

EMMA

You've misunderstood me.

JERRY

Have I? How?

EMMA

Well, quite simply, you often do meet, or have lunch, to discuss a particular writer or a particular book, don't you? So to those meetings, or lunches, there is a point or a subject.

JERRY

Well, there isn't to this one.

Pause

EMMA

You haven't discovered any new writers, while I've been away?

JERRY

No. Sam fell off his bike.

EMMA

No.

JERRY

He was knocked out. He was out for about a minute.

EMMA

Were you with him?

JERRY

No. Judith. He's all right. And then I got this bug.

EMMA

Oh dear.

JERRY

So I've had time for nothing.

EMMA

Everything will be better, now I'm back.

JERRY

Yes.

EMMA

Oh, I read that Spinks, the book you gave me.

JERRY

What do you think?

EMMA

Excellent.

JERRY

Robert hated it. He wouldn't publish it.

EMMA

What's he like?

JERRY

Who?

EMMA

Spinks.

JERRY

Spinks? He's a very thin bloke. About fifty. Wears dark glasses day and night. He lives alone, in a furnished room. Quite like this one, actually. He's ... unfussed.

EMMA

Furnished rooms suit him?

JERRY

Yes.

EMMA

They suit me too. And you? Do you still like it? Our home?

JERRY

It's marvellous not to have a telephone.

EMMA

And marvellous to have me?

JERRY

You're all right.

EMMA

I cook and slave for you.

JERRY

You do.

EMMA

I bought something in Venice – for the house.

She opens the parcel, takes out a tablecloth. Puts it on the table.

Do you like it?

JERRY

It's lovely.

Pause

                    EMMA

Do you think we'll ever go to Venice together?

Pause

No. Probably not.

Pause

                    JERRY

You don't think I should see Robert for lunch on Thursday,
or on Friday, for that matter?

                    EMMA

Why do you say that?

                    JERRY

You don't think I should see him at all?

                    EMMA

I didn't say that. How can you not see him? Don't be silly.

Pause

                    JERRY

I had a terrible panic when you were away. I was sorting out a
contract, in my office, with some lawyers. I suddenly
couldn't remember what I'd done with your letter. I couldn't
remember putting it in the safe. I said I had to look for
something in the safe. I opened the safe. It wasn't there. I had
to go on with the damn contract ... I kept seeing it lying
somewhere in the house, being picked up ...

EMMA

Did you find it?

JERRY

It was in the pocket of a jacket – in my wardrobe – at home.

EMMA

God.

JERRY

Something else happened a few months ago – I didn't tell you. We had a drink one evening. Well, we had our drink, and I got home about eight, walked in the door, Judith said, hello, you're a bit late. Sorry, I said, I was having a drink with Spinks. Spinks? she said, how odd, he's just phoned, five minutes ago, wanted to speak to you, he didn't mention he'd just seen you. You know old Spinks, I said, not exactly forthcoming, is he? He'd probably remembered something he'd meant to say but hadn't. I'll ring him later. I went up to see the kids and then we all had dinner.

Pause

Listen. Do you remember, when was it, a few years ago, we were all in your kitchen, must have been Christmas or something, do you remember, all the kids were running about and suddenly I picked Charlotte up and lifted her high up, high up, and then down and up. Do you remember how she laughed?

EMMA

Everyone laughed.

JERRY

She was so light. And there was your husband and my wife

and all the kids, all standing and laughing in your kitchen. I
can't get rid of it.

                            EMMA
It was your kitchen, actually.

He takes her hand. They stand. They go to the bed and lie down.

Why shouldn't you throw her up?

She caresses him. They embrace.

1973 Later

Scene Seven

Restaurant. 1973. Summer.

ROBERT *at table drinking white wine. The* WAITER *brings* JERRY *to the table.* JERRY *sits.*

JERRY

Hullo, Robert.

ROBERT

Hullo.

JERRY (*to the* WAITER)

I'd like a Scotch on the rocks.

WAITER

With water?

JERRY

What?

WAITER

You want it with water?

JERRY

No. No water. Just on the rocks.

WAITER

Certainly signore.

ROBERT

Scotch? You don't usually drink Scotch at lunchtime.

JERRY

I've had a bug, actually.

ROBERT

Ah.

JERRY

And the only thing to get rid of this bug was Scotch – at
lunchtime as well as at night. So I'm still drinking Scotch at
lunchtime in case it comes back.

ROBERT

Like an apple a day.

JERRY

Precisely.

WAITER *brings Scotch on rocks.*

Cheers.

ROBERT

Cheers.

WAITER

The menus, signori.

He passes the menus, goes.

ROBERT

How are you? Apart from the bug?

JERRY

Fine.

ROBERT

Ready for some squash?

JERRY

When I've got rid of the bug, yes.

ROBERT

I thought you had got rid of it.

JERRY

Why do you think I'm still drinking Scotch at lunchtime?

ROBERT

Oh yes. We really must play. We haven't played for years.

JERRY

How old are you now, then?

ROBERT

Thirty six.

JERRY

That means I'm thirty six as well.

ROBERT

If you're a day.

JERRY

Bit violent, squash.

ROBERT

Ring me. We'll have a game.

JERRY

How was Venice?

WAITER

Ready to order, signori?

ROBERT

What'll you have?

JERRY *looks at him, briefly, then back to the menu.*

JERRY

I'll have melone. And Piccata al limone with a green salad.

WAITER

Insalate verde. Prosciutto e melone?

JERRY

No. Just melone. On the rocks.

ROBERT

I'll have prosciutto and melone. Fried scampi. And spinach.

WAITER

E spinaci. Grazie, signore.

ROBERT

And a bottle of Corvo Bianco straight away.

WAITER

Si, signore. Molte grazies. (*He goes.*)

JERRY

Is he the one who's always been here or is it his son?

ROBERT

You mean has his son always been here?

JERRY

No, is *he* his son? I mean, is he the son of the one who's always been here?

ROBERT

No, he's his father.

JERRY

Ah. Is he?

ROBERT

He's the one who speaks wonderful Italian.

JERRY

Yes. Your Italian's pretty good, isn't it?

ROBERT

No. Not at all.

JERRY

Yes it is.

ROBERT

No, it's Emma's Italian which is very good. Emma's Italian is very good.

JERRY

Is it? I didn't know that.

WAITER *with bottle*.

WAITER
Corvo Bianco, signore.

ROBERT
Thank you.

JERRY
How was it, anyway? Venice.

WAITER
Venice, signore? Beautiful. A most beautiful place of Italy.
You see that painting on the wall? Is Venice.

ROBERT
So it is.

WAITER
You know what is none of in Venice?

JERRY
What?

WAITER
Traffico.

He goes, smiling.

ROBERT
Cheers.

JERRY
Cheers.

ROBERT

When were you last there?

JERRY

Oh, years.

ROBERT

How's Judith?

JERRY

What? Oh, you know, okay. Busy.

ROBERT

And the kids?

JERRY

All right. Sam fell off –

ROBERT

What?

JERRY

No, no, nothing. So how was it?

ROBERT

You used to go there with Judith, didn't you?

JERRY

Yes, but we haven't been there for years.

Pause

How about Charlotte? Did she enjoy it?

ROBERT

I think she did.

Pause

I did.

JERRY

Good.

ROBERT

I went for a trip to Torcello.

JERRY

Oh, really? Lovely place.

ROBERT

Incredible day. I got up very early and – whoomp – right across the lagoon – to Torcello. Not a soul stirring.

JERRY

What's the 'whoomp'?

ROBERT

Speedboat.

JERRY

Ah. I thought –

ROBERT

What?

JERRY

It's so long ago, I'm obviously wrong. I thought one went to Torcello by gondola.

ROBERT

It would take hours. No, no, – whoomp – across the lagoon in the dawn.

JERRY

Sounds good.

ROBERT

I was quite alone.

JERRY

Where was Emma?

ROBERT

I think asleep.

JERRY

Ah.

ROBERT

I was alone for hours, as a matter of fact, on the island. Highpoint, actually, of the whole trip.

JERRY

Was it? Well, it sounds marvellous.

ROBERT

Yes. I sat on the grass and read Yeats.

JERRY

Yeats on Torcello?

ROBERT

They went well together.

WAITER *with food*.

WAITER
One melone. One prosciutto e melone.

ROBERT
Prosciutto for me.

WAITER
Buon appetito.

ROBERT
Emma read that novel of that chum of yours – what's his name?

JERRY
I don't know. What?

ROBERT
Spinks.

JERRY
Oh Spinks. Yes. The one you didn't like.

ROBERT
The one I wouldn't publish.

JERRY
I remember. Did Emma like it?

ROBERT
She seemed to be madly in love with it.

JERRY
Good.

ROBERT

You like it yourself, do you?

JERRY

I do.

ROBERT

And it's very successful?

JERRY

It is.

ROBERT

Tell me, do you think that makes me a publisher of unique critical judgement or a foolish publisher?

JERRY

A foolish publisher.

ROBERT

I agree with you. I am a very foolish publisher.

JERRY

No you're not. What are you talking about? You're a good publisher. What are you talking about?

ROBERT

I'm a bad publisher because I hate books. Or to be more precise, prose. Or to be even more precise, modern prose, I mean modern novels, first novels and second novels, all that promise and sensibility it falls upon me to judge, to put the firm's money on, and then to push for the third novel, see it

done, see the dust jacket done, see the dinner for the national
literary editors done, see the signing in Hatchards done, see
the lucky author cook himself to death, all in the name of
literature. You know what you and Emma have in common?
You love literature. I mean you love modern prose literature.
I mean you love the new novel by the new Casey or Spinks. It
gives you both a thrill.

JERRY

You must be pissed.

ROBERT

Really? You mean you don't think it gives Emma a thrill?

JERRY

How do I know? She's your wife.

Pause

ROBERT

Yes. Yes. You're quite right. I shouldn't have to consult you.
I shouldn't have to consult anyone.

JERRY

I'd like some more wine.

ROBERT

Yes, yes. Waiter! Another bottle of Corvo Bianco. And
where's our lunch? This place is going to pot. Mind you, it's
worse in Venice. They really don't give a fuck there. I'm not
drunk. You can't get drunk on Corvo Bianco. Mind you . . .
last night . . . I was up late . . . I hate brandy . . . it stinks of
modern literature. No, look, I'm sorry . . .

WAITER *with bottle*.

WAITER
Corvo Bianco.

ROBERT
Same glass. Where's our lunch?

WAITER
It comes.

ROBERT
I'll pour.

WAITER *goes, with melon plates*.

No, look, I'm sorry, have another drink. I'll tell you what it is, it's just that I can't bear being back in London. I was happy, such a rare thing, not in Venice, I don't mean that, I mean on Torcello, when I walked about Torcello in the early morning, alone, I was happy, I wanted to stay there forever.

JERRY
We all . . .

ROBERT
Yes, we all . . . feel that sometimes. Oh you do yourself, do you?

Pause

I mean there's nothing really wrong, you see. I've got the family. Emma and I are very good together. I think the world of her. And I actually consider Casey to be a first rate writer.

JERRY

Do you really?

ROBERT

First rate. I'm proud to publish him and you discovered him and that was very clever of you.

JERRY

Thanks.

ROBERT

You've got a good nose and you care and I respect that in you. So does Emma. We often talk about it.

JERRY

How is Emma?

ROBERT

Very well. You must come and have a drink sometime. She'd love to see you.

1971

Scene Eight

Flat. 1971. Summer.

Flat empty. Kitchen door open. Table set; crockery, glasses, bottle of wine.

JERRY comes in through front door, with key.

JERRY

Hullo.

EMMA's voice from kitchen.

EMMA

Hullo.

EMMA comes out of kitchen. She is wearing an apron.

EMMA

I've only just got here. I meant to be here ages ago. I'm making this stew. It'll be hours.

He kisses her.

Are you starving?

JERRY

Yes.

He kisses her.

EMMA

No really. I'll never do it. You sit down. I'll get it on.

JERRY

What a lovely apron.

EMMA

Good.

She kisses him, goes into kitchen.
She calls. He pours wine.

EMMA

What have you been doing?

JERRY

Just walked through the park.

EMMA

What was it like?

JERRY

Beautiful. Empty. A slight mist.

Pause

I sat down for a bit, under a tree. It was very quiet. I jus
looked at the Serpentine.

Pause

EMMA

And then?

JERRY

Then I got a taxi to Wessex Grove. Number 31. And I climbed the steps and opened the front door and then climbed the stairs and opened this door and found you in a new apron cooking a stew.

EMMA *comes out of the kitchen.*

EMMA

It's on.

JERRY

Which is now on.

EMMA *pours herself a vodka.*

JERRY

Vodka? At lunchtime?

EMMA

Just feel like one.

She drinks.

I ran into Judith yesterday. Did she tell you?

JERRY

No, she didn't.

Pause

Where?

EMMA

Lunch.

JERRY

Lunch?

EMMA

She didn't tell you?

JERRY

No.

EMMA

That's funny.

JERRY

What do you mean, lunch? Where?

EMMA

At Fortnum and Mason's.

JERRY

Fortnum and Mason's? What the hell was she doing a
Fortnum and Mason's?

EMMA

She was lunching with a lady.

JERRY

A lady?

EMMA

Yes.

Pause

JERRY

Fortnum and Mason's is a long way from the hospital.

EMMA

Of course it isn't.

JERRY

Well ... I suppose not.

Pause

And you?

EMMA

Me?

JERRY

What were you doing at Fortnum and Mason's?

EMMA

Lunching with my sister.

JERRY

Ah.

Pause

EMMA

Judith ... didn't tell you?

JERRY

I haven't really seen her. I was out late last night, with Casey.
And she was out early this morning.

Pause

EMMA

Do you think she knows?

JERRY

Knows?

EMMA

Does she know? About us?

JERRY

No.

EMMA

Are you sure?

JERRY

She's too busy. At the hospital. And then the kids. Sh
doesn't go in for ... speculation.

EMMA

But what about clues? Isn't she interested ... to follow clues

JERRY

What clues?

EMMA

Well, there must be some ... available to her ... to pick up

JERRY

There are none ... available to her.

EMMA

Oh. Well ... good.

Pause

JERRY

She has an admirer.

EMMA

Really?

JERRY

Another doctor. He takes her for drinks. It's . . . irritating. I mean, she says that's all there is to it. He likes her, she's fond of him, etcetera, etcetera . . . perhaps that's what I find irritating. I don't know exactly what's going on.

EMMA

Oh, why shouldn't she have an admirer? I have an admirer.

JERRY

Who?

EMMA

Uuh . . . you, I think.

JERRY

Ah. Yes.

He takes her hand.

I'm more than that.

Pause

EMMA

Tell me . . . have you ever thought . . . of changing your life?

JERRY

Changing?

EMMA

Mmnn.

Pause

JERRY

It's impossible.

Pause

EMMA

Do you think she's being unfaithful to you?

JERRY

No. I don't know.

EMMA

When you were in America, just now, for instance?

JERRY

No.

EMMA

Have you ever been unfaithful?

JERRY

To whom?

EMMA

To me, of course.

JERRY

No.

Pause

Have you ... to me?

EMMA

No.

Pause

If she was, what would you do?

JERRY

She isn't. She's busy. She's got lots to do. She's a very good doctor. She likes her life. She loves the kids.

EMMA

Ah.

JERRY

She loves me.

Pause

EMMA

Ah.

Silence

JERRY

All that means something.

EMMA

It certainly does.

JERRY

But I adore you.

Pause

I adore you.

EMMA *takes his hand.*

                    EMMA
Yes.

Pause

Listen. There's something I have to tell you.

                    JERRY
What?

                    EMMA
I'm pregnant. It was when you were in America.

Pause

It wasn't anyone else. It was my husband.

Pause

                    JERRY
Yes. Yes, of course.

Pause

I'm very happy for you.

1968

Scene Nine

Robert and Emma's House. Bedroom. 1968. Winter.

The room is dimly lit. JERRY *is sitting in the shadows. Faint music through the door.*

The door opens. Light. Music. EMMA *comes in, closes the door. She goes towards the mirror, sees* JERRY.

EMMA

Good God.

JERRY

I've been waiting for you.

EMMA

What do you mean?

JERRY

I knew you'd come.

He drinks.

EMMA

I've just come in to comb my hair.

He stands.

JERRY

I knew you'd have to. I knew you'd have to comb your hair.
knew you'd have to get away from the party.

She goes to the mirror, combs her hair.
He watches her.

You're a beautiful hostess.

EMMA

Aren't you enjoying the party?

JERRY

You're beautiful.

He goes to her.

Listen. I've been watching you all night. I must tell you,
want to tell you, I have to tell you –

EMMA

Please –

JERRY

You're incredible.

EMMA

You're drunk.

JERRY

Nevertheless.

He holds her.

EMMA

Jerry.

JERRY

I was best man at your wedding. I saw you in white. I watched
you glide by in white.

EMMA

I wasn't in white.

JERRY

You know what should have happened?

EMMA

What?

JERRY

I should have had you, in your white, before the wedding. I
should have blackened you, in your white wedding dress,
blackened you in your bridal dress, before ushering you into
your wedding, as your best man.

EMMA

My husband's best man. Your best friend's best man.

JERRY

No. Your best man.

EMMA

I must get back.

JERRY

You're lovely. I'm crazy about you. All these words I'm
using, don't you see, they've never been said before. Can't

you see? I'm crazy about you. It's a whirlwind. Have you ever been to the Sahara Desert? Listen to me. It's true. Listen. You overwhelm me. You're so lovely.

EMMA

I'm not.

JERRY

You're so beautiful. Look at the way you look at me.

EMMA

I'm not . . . looking at you.

JERRY

Look at the way you're looking at me. I can't wait for you, I'm bowled over, I'm totally knocked out, you dazzle me, you jewel, my jewel, I can't ever sleep again, no, listen, it's the truth, I won't walk, I'll be a cripple, I'll descend, I'll diminish, into total paralysis, my life is in your hands, that's what you're banishing me to, a state of catatonia, do you know the state of catatonia? do you? do you? the state of . . . where the reigning prince is the prince of emptiness, the prince of absence, the prince of desolation. I love you.

EMMA

My husband is at the other side of that door.

JERRY

Everyone knows. The world knows. It knows. But they'll never know, they'll never know, they're in a different world. I adore you. I'm madly in love with you. I can't believe that what anyone is at this moment saying has ever happened has ever happened. Nothing has ever happened. Nothing. This is

the only thing that has ever happened. Your eyes kill me. I'm
lost. You're wonderful.

EMMA

No.

JERRY

Yes.

He kisses her.
She breaks away.
He kisses her.

Laughter off.
She breaks away.
Door opens. ROBERT.

EMMA

Your best friend is drunk.

JERRY

As you are my best and oldest friend and, in the present
instance, my host, I decided to take this opportunity to tell
your wife how beautiful she was.

ROBERT

Quite right.

JERRY

It is quite right, to . . . to face up to the facts . . . and to offer a
token, without blush, a token of one's unalloyed appreci-
ation, no holds barred.

ROBERT

Absolutely.

JERRY

And how wonderful for you that this is so, that this is th
case, that her beauty is the case.

ROBERT

Quite right.

JERRY *moves to* ROBERT *and takes hold of his elbow.*

JERRY

I speak as your oldest friend. Your best man.

ROBERT

You are, actually.

He clasps JERRY's *shoulder, briefly, turns, leaves the room.*

EMMA *moves towards the door.* JERRY *grasps her arm.*
She stops still.

They stand still, looking at each other.

Monologue

Monologue was first televised on BBC–TV on 13 April 1973.

MAN   Henry Woolf

Directed by Christopher Morahan

Man alone in a chair.
He refers to another chair, which is empty.

MAN

I think I'll nip down to the games room. Stretch my legs. Have
a game of ping pong. What about you? Fancy a game? How
would you like a categorical thrashing? I'm willing to accept
any challenge, any stakes, any gauntlet you'd care to fling
down. What have you done with your gauntlets, by the way?
In fact, *while we're at it*, what happened to your motorbike?

Pause

You looked bold in black. The only thing I didn't like was
your face, too white, the face, stuck between your black hel-
met and your black hair and your black motoring jacket, kind
of aghast, blatantly vulnerable, veering towards pitiful. Of
course, you weren't cut out to be a motorbikist, it went against
your nature, I never understood what you were getting at.
What is certain is that it didn't work, it never convinced me,
it never got you onto any top shelf with me. You should have
been black, you should have had a black face, then you'd be
getting somewhere, really making a go of it.

Pause

I often had the impression ... often ... that you two were
actually brother and sister, some kind of link-up, some kind of
identical shimmer, deep down in your characters, an inkling,

no more, that at one time you had shared the same pot. But of
course she was black. Black as the Ace of Spades. And a life-
lover, to boot.

Pause

All the same, you and I, even then, never mind the weather,
weren't we, we were always available for net practice, at the
drop of a hat, or a game of fives, or a walk and talk through
the park, or a couple of rounds of putting before lunch, given
fair to moderate conditions, and no burdensome commitments.

Pause

The thing I like, I mean quite immeasurably, is this kind of
conversation, this kind of exchange, this class of mutual
reminiscence.

Pause

Sometimes I think you've forgotten the black girl, the ebony
one. Sometimes I think you've forgotten me.

Pause

You haven't forgotten *me*. Who was your best mate, who was
your truest mate? You introduced me to Webster and Tour-
neur, admitted, but who got you going on Tristan Tzara,
Breton, Giacometti and all that lot? Not to mention Louis
Ferdinand Céline, now out of favour. And John Dos. Who
bought you both all those custard tins cut price? I say both. I
was the best friend either of you ever had and I'm still prepared to prove it, I'm still prepared to wrap my braces round
anyone's neck, in your defence.

Pause

Now you're going to say you loved her soul and I loved her body. You're going to trot that old one out. I know you were much more beautiful than me, much more *aquiline*, I know *that*, that I'll give you, more *ethereal*, more thoughtful, *slyer*, while I had both feet firmly planted on the deck. But I'll tell you one thing you don't know. She loved my soul. It was my soul she loved.

Pause

You never say what you're ready for now. You're not even ready for a game of ping pong. You're incapable of saying of what it is you're capable, where your relish lies, where you're sharp, excited, why you never are capable . . . never are . . . capable of exercising a crisp and fullbodied appraisal of the buzzing possibilities of your buzzing brain cells. You often, I'll be frank, act as if you're dead, as if the Balls Pond Road and the lovely ebony lady never existed, as if the rain in the light on the pavements in the twilight never existed, as if our sporting and intellectual life never was.

Pause

She was tired. She sat down. She was tired. The journey. The rush hour. The weather, so unpredictable. She'd put on a woollen dress because the morning was chilly, but the day had changed, totally, totally changed. She cried. You jumped up like a . . . those things, forget the name, monkey on a box, *jack in a box*, held her hand, made her tea, a rare burst. Perhaps the change in the weather had gone to your head.

Pause

I loved her body. Not that, between ourselves, it's one way or another a thing of any importance. My spasms could be your spasms. Who's to tell or care?

Pause

Well . . . she did . . . can . . . could . . .

Pause

We all walked, arm in arm, through the long grass, over the bridge, sat outside the pub in the sun by the river, the pub was shut.

Pause

Did anyone notice us? Did you see anyone looking at us?

Pause

Touch my body, she said to you. You did. Of course you did. You'd be a bloody fool if you didn't. You'd have been a bloody fool if you hadn't. It was perfectly *normal*.

Pause

That was behind the partition.

Pause

I brought her to see you, after you'd pissed off to live in Notting Hill Gate. Naturally. They all end up there. I'll never end up there, I'll never end up on that side of the Park

Pause

Sitting there with your record player, growing bald, Beethoven, cocoa, cats. That really dates it. The cocoa dates it. It was your detachment was dangerous. I knew it of course like the back of my hand. That was the web my darling black darling hovered in, wavered in, my black *moth*. She stuttered in that light, your slightly sullen, non-committal, deadly dangerous light. But it's a fact of life. The ones that keep silent are the best off.

Pause

As for me, I've always liked simple love scenes, the classic set-ups, the sweet . . . the sweet . . . the sweet farewell at Paddington station. My collar turned up. Her soft cheeks. Standing close to me, legs under her raincoat, the platform, her cheeks, her hands, nothing like the sound of steam to keep love warm, to keep it moist, to bring it to the throat, my ebony love, she smiles at me, I touched her.

Pause

I feel for you. Even if you feel nothing . . . for me. I feel for you, old chap.

Pause

I keep busy in the *mind*, and that's why I'm still sparking, get it? I've got a hundred per cent more energy in me now than when I was twenty-two. When I was twenty-two I slept twenty-four hours a day. And twenty-two hours a day at twenty-four. Work it out for yourself. But now I'm sparking, at my peak, *up here*, two thousand revolutions a second, every living hour of the day and night. I'm a front runner. My watchword is vigilance. I'm way past mythologies, left them all behind, cocoa, sleep, Beethoven, cats, rain, black girls, bosom pals, literature, custard. You'll say I've been talking about nothing else all night, but can't you see, you bloody fool, that I can *afford* to do it, can't you appreciate the irony? Even if you're too dim to catch the irony in the words themselves, the words I have chosen myself, quite scrupulously, and with intent, you can't miss the irony in the tone of *voice*!

Pause

What you are in fact witnessing is freedom. I no longer participate in holy ceremony. The crap is cut.

Silence

You should have had a black face, that was your mistake. You could have made a going concern out of it, you could have chalked it up in the book, you could have had two black kids.

Pause

I'd have died for them.

Pause
I'd have been their uncle.

Pause

I am their uncle.

Pause

I'm your children's uncle.

Pause

I'll take them out, tell them jokes.

Pause

I love your children.

Family Voices

Family Voices was first broadcast on BBC Radio 3 on 22 January 1981, with the following cast:

VOICE 1, *a young man*   Michael Kitchen
VOICE 2, *a woman*   Peggy Ashcroft
VOICE 3, *a man*   Mark Dignam

Directed by Peter Hall

Family Voices was subsequently presented in a 'platform performance' by the National Theatre, London, on 1 February 1981. Cast and director were the same. The decor was by John Bury.

I am having a very nice time.

The weather is up and down, but surprisingly warm, on the whole, more often than not.

I hope you're feeling well, and not as peaky as you did, the last time I saw you.

No, you didn't feel peaky, you felt perfectly well, you simply looked peaky.

Do you miss me?

I am having a very nice time and I hope you are glad of that.

At the moment I am dead drunk.

I had five pints in The Fishmongers Arms tonight, followed by three double scotches, and literally rolled home.

When I say home I can assure you that my room is extremely pleasant. So is the bathroom. Extremely pleasant. I have some very pleasant baths indeed in the bathroom. So does everybody else in the house. They all lie quite naked in the bath and have very pleasant baths indeed. All the people in the house go about saying what a superb bath and bathroom the one we share is, they go about telling literally everyone they meet what lovely baths you can get in this place, more or less unparalleled, to put it bluntly.

It's got a lot to do with the landlady, who is a Mrs Withers, a person who turns out to be an utterly charming person, of impeccable credentials.

When I said I was drunk I was of course making a joke.

I bet you laughed.

Mother?

Did you get the joke? You know I never touch alcohol.

I like being in this enormous city, all by myself. I expect to make friends in the not too distant future.

I expect to make girlfriends too.

I expect to meet a very nice girl. Having met her, I shall bring her home to meet my mother.

I like walking in this enormous city, all by myself. It's fun to know no-one at all. When I pass people in the street they don't realise that I don't know them from Adam. They know other people and even more other people know them, so they naturally think that even if I don't know them I know the other people. So they look at me, they try to catch my eye, they expect me to speak. But as I do not know them I do not speak. Nor do I ever feel the slightest temptation to do so.

You see, mother, I am not lonely, because all that has ever happened to me is with me, keeps me company; my childhood, for example, through which you, my mother, and he, my father, guided me.

I get on very well with my landlady, Mrs Withers. She tells me
I am her solace. I have a drink with her at lunchtime and
another one at teatime and then take her for a couple in the
evening at The Fishmongers Arms.

She was in the Women's Air Force in the Second World War.
Don't drop a bollock, Charlie, she's fond of saying, Call him
Flight Sergeant and he'll be happy as a pig in shit.

You'd really like her, mother.

I think it's dawn. I can see it coming up. Another day. A day
I warmly welcome. And so I shall end this letter to you, my
dear mother, with my love.

VOICE 2

Darling. Where are you? The flowers are wonderful here. The
blooms. You so loved them. Why do you never write?

I think of you and wonder how you are. Do you ever think of
me? Your mother? Ever? At all?

Have you changed your address?

Have you made friends with anyone? A nice boy? Or a nice
girl?

There are so many nice boys and nice girls about. But please
don't get mixed up with the other sort. They can land you in
such terrible trouble. And you'd hate it so. You're so scrupu-
lous, so particular.

I often think that I would love to live happily ever after with
you and your young wife. And she would be such a lovely wife

to you and I would have the occasional dinner with you both. A dinner I would be quite happy to cook myself, should you both be tired after your long day, as I'm sure you will be.

I sometimes walk the cliff path and think of you. I think of the times you walked the cliff path, with your father, with cheese sandwiches. Didn't you? You both sat on the clifftop and ate my cheese sandwiches together. Do you remember our little joke? Munch, munch. We had a damn good walk, your father would say. You mean you had a good munch munch, I would say. And you would both laugh.

Darling. I miss you. I gave birth to you. Where are you?

I wrote to you three months ago, telling you of your father's death. Did you receive my letter?

VOICE 1
I'm not at all sure that I like the people in this house, apart from Mrs Withers and her daughter, Jane. Jane is a schoolgirl who works hard at her homework.

She keeps her nose to the grindstone. This I find impressive. There's not too much of that about these days. But I'm not so sure about the other people in this house.

One is an old man.

The one who is an old man retires early. He is bald.

The other is a woman who wears red dresses.

The other one is another man.

He is big. He is much bigger than the other man. His hair is black. He has black eyebrows and black hair on the back of his hands.

I ask Mrs Withers about them but she will talk of nothing but her days in the Women's Air Force in the Second World War.

I have decided that Jane is not Mrs Withers' daughter but her grand-daughter. Mrs Withers is seventy. Jane is fifteen. That I am convinced is the truth.

At night I hear whispering from the other rooms and do not understand it. I hear steps on the stairs but do not dare go out to investigate.

VOICE 2

As your father grew closer to his death he spoke more and more of you, with tenderness and bewilderment. I consoled him with the idea that you had left home to make him proud of you. I think I succeeded in this. One of his last sentences was: Give him a slap on the back from me. Give him a slap on the back from me.

VOICE I

I have made a remarkable discovery. The old man who is bald and who retires early is named Withers. Benjamin Withers. Unless it is simply a coincidence it must mean that he is a relation.

I asked Mrs Withers what the truth of this was. She poured herself a gin and looked at it before she drank it. Then she looked at me and said: You are my little pet. I've always wanted a little pet but I've never had one and now I've got one.

Sometimes she gives me a cuddle, as if she were my mother.

But I haven't forgotten that I have a mother and that you are my mother.

Sometimes I wonder if you remember that you have a mother.

Something has happened. The woman who wears red dresses stopped me and asked me into her room for a cup of tea. I went into her room. It was far bigger than I had expected, with sofas and curtains and veils and shrouds and rugs and soft material all over the walls, dark blue. Jane was sitting on a sofa doing her homework, by the look of it. I was invited to sit on the same sofa. Tea had already been made and stood ready, in a china teaset, of a most elegant design. I was given a cup. So was Jane, who smiled at me. I haven't introduced myself, the woman said, my name is Lady Withers. Jane sipped her tea with her legs up on the sofa. Her stockinged toes came to rest on my thigh. It wasn't the biggest sofa in the world. Lady Withers sat opposite us on a substantially bigger sofa. Her dress, I decided, wasn't red but pink. Jane was in green, apart from her toes, which were clad in black. Lady Withers asked me about you, mother. She asked me about my mother. I said, with absolute conviction, that you were the best mother in the world. She asked me to call her Lally. And to call Jane Jane. I said I did call Jane Jane. Jane gave me a bun. I think it was a bun. Lady Withers bit into her bun. Jane bit into her bun, her toes now resting on my lap. Lady Withers seemed to be enjoying her bun, on her sofa. She finished it and picked up another. I had never seen so many buns. One quick glance told me they were perched on cakestands, all over the room. Lady Withers went through her second bun with no trouble at all and was at once on to another. Jane, on the other hand, chewed almost dreamily at her bun and when a currant was left stranded on her upper lip she licked it off, without haste. I could not reconcile this with the fact that her toes were quite restless, even agitated. Her mouth, eating, was measured, serene; her toes, not eating, were agitated, highly strung, some would say hysterical. My bun turned out to be rock solid. I bit into it, it jumped out of my mouth and bounced into my lap. Jane's feet caught it. It calmed her toes down. She juggled the bun, with some expertise, along them. I recalled that, in an early exchange between us, she had told me she wanted to be an acrobat.

VOICE 2

Darling. Where are you? Why do you never write? Nobody knows your whereabouts. Nobody knows if you are alive or dead. Nobody can find you. Have you changed your name?

If you are alive you are a monster. On his deathbed your father cursed you. He cursed me too, to tell the truth. He cursed everyone in sight. Except that you were not in sight. I do not blame you entirely for your father's ill humour, but your absence and silence were a great burden on him, a weariness to him. He died in lamentation and oath. Was that your wish? Now I am alone, apart from Millie, who sometimes comes over from Dover. She is some consolation. Her eyes well with tears when she speaks of you, your dear sister's eyes well with tears. She has made a truly happy marriage and has a lovely little boy. When he is older he will want to know where his uncle is. What shall we say?

Or perhaps you will arrive here in a handsome new car, one day, in the not too distant future, in a nice new suit, quite out of the blue, and hold me in your arms.

VOICE I

Lady Withers stood up. As Jane is doing her homework, she said, perhaps you would care to leave and come again another day. Jane withdrew her feet, my bun clasped between her two big toes. Yes of course, I said, unless Jane would like me to help her with her homework. No thank you, said Lady Withers, I shall help her with her homework.

What I didn't say is that I am thinking of offering myself out as a tutor. I consider that I would make an excellent tutor, to the young, in any one of a number of subjects. Jane would be an ideal pupil. She possesses a true love of learning. That is the sense of her one takes from her every breath, her every sigh and exhalation. When she turns her eyes upon you you see within her eyes, raw, untutored, unexercised but willing, a deep love of learning.

These are midnight thoughts, mother, although the time is ten twenty-three, precisely.

VOICE 2

Darling?

VOICE I

While I was lying in my bath this afternoon, thinking on these things, there was apparently a knock on the front door. The man with black hair apparently opened the door. Two women stood on the doorstep. They said they were my mother and my sister, and asked for me. He denied knowledge of me. No, he had not heard of me. No, there was no-one of that name resident. This was a family house, no strangers admitted. No, they got on very well, thank you very much, without intruders. I suggest, he said, that you both go back to where you come from, and stop bothering innocent hardworking people with

your slanders and your libels, these all too predictable
excrescences of the depraved mind at the end of its tether. I
can smell your sort a mile off and I am quite prepared to put
you both on a charge of malicious mischief, insulting behaviour
and vagabondage, in other words wandering around on door-
steps knowingly, without any visible means of support. So
piss off out of it before I call a copper.

I was lying in my bath when the door opened. I thought I had
locked it. My name's Riley, he said, How's the bath? Very
nice, I said. You've got a wellknit yet slender frame, he said,
I thought you only a snip, I never imagined you would be as
wellknit and slender as I now see you are. Oh thank you, I
said. Don't thank me, he said, It's God you have to thank. Or
your mother. I've just dismissed a couple of imposters at the
front door. We'll get no more shit from that quarter. He then
sat on the edge of the bath and recounted to me what I've
just recounted to you.

It interests me that my father wasn't bothered to make the
trip.

VOICE 2

I hear your father's step on the stair. I hear his cough. But
his step and his cough fade. He does not open the door.

Sometimes I think I have always been sitting like this. I sometimes think I have always been sitting like this, alone by an
indifferent fire, curtains closed, night, winter.

You see, I have my thoughts too. Thoughts no-one else knows
I have, thoughts none of my family ever knew I had. But I
write of them to you now, wherever you are.

What I mean is that when, for example, I was washing your hair, with the most delicate shampoo, and rinsing, and then drying your hair so gently with my soft towel, so that no murmur came from you, of discomfort or unease, and then looked into your eyes, and saw you look into mine, knowing that you wanted no-one else, no-one at all, knowing that you were entirely happy in my arms, I knew also, for example, that I was at the same time sitting by an indifferent fire, alone in winter, in eternal night without you.

VOICE I

Lady Withers plays the piano. They were sitting, the three women, about the room. About the room were bottles of a vin rosé, of a pink I shall never forget. They sipped their wine from such lovely glass, an elegance of gesture and grace I thought long dead. Lady Withers wore a necklace around her alabaster neck, a neck amazingly young. She played Schumann. She smiled at me. Mrs Withers and Jane smiled at me. I took a seat. I took it and sat in it. I am in it. I will never leave it.

Oh mother, I have found my home, my family. Little did I ever dream I could know such happiness.

VOICE 2

Perhaps I should forget all about you. Perhaps I should curse you as your father cursed you. Oh I pray, I pray your life is a torment to you. I wait for your letter begging me to come to you. I'll spit on it.

VOICE I

Mother, mother, I've had the most unpleasant, the most mystifying encounter, with the man who calls himself Mr Withers. Will you give me your advice?

Come in here, son, he called. Look sharp. Don't mess about.

I haven't got all night. I went in. A jug. A basin. A bicycle.

You know where you are? he said. You're in my room. It's not Euston station. Get me? It's a true oasis.

This is the only room in this house where you can pick up a caravanserai to all points West. Compris? Comprende? Get me? Are you prepared to follow me down the mountain? Look at me. My name's Withers. I'm there or thereabouts. Follow? Embargo on all duff terminology. With me? Embargo on all things redundant. All areas in that connection verboten. You're in a diseaseridden land, boxer. Keep your weight on all the left feet you can lay your hands on. Keep dancing. The old foxtrot is the classical response but that's not the response I'm talking about. Nor am I talking about the other response. Up the slaves. Get me? This is a place of creatures, up and down stairs. Creatures of the rhythmic splits, the rhythmic sideswipes, the rums and roulettes, the macaroni tatters, the dumplings in jam mayonnaise, a catapulting ordure of gross and ramshackle shenanigans, openended paraphernalia. Follow me? It all adds up. It's before you and behind you. I'm the only saviour of the grace you find yourself wanting in. Mind how you go. Look sharp. Get my drift? Don't let it get too mouldy. Watch the mould. Get the feel of it, sonny, get the density. Look at me.

And I did.

VOICE 2
I am ill.

VOICE 1
It was like looking into a pit of molten lava, mother. One look was enough for me.

VOICE 2

Come to me.

VOICE I

I joined Mrs Withers for a Campari and soda in the kitchen. She spoke of her youth. I was a right titbit, she said. I was like a piece of plum duff. They used to come from miles to try their luck. I fell head over heels with a man in the Fleet Air Arm. He adored me. They had him murdered because they didn't want us to know happiness. I could have married him and had tons of sons. But oh no. He went down with his ship. I heard it on the wireless.

VOICE 2

I wait for you.

VOICE I

Later that night Riley and I shared a cup of cocoa in his quarters. I like slender lads, Riley said. Slender but strong. I've never made any secret of it. But I've had to restrain myself, I've had to keep a tight rein on my inclinations. That's because my deepest disposition is towards religion. I've always been a deeply religious man. You can imagine the tension this creates in my soul. I walk about in a constant state of spiritual, emotional, psychological and physical tension. It's breathtaking, the discipline I'm called upon to exert. My lust is unimaginably violent but it goes against my best interests, which are to keep on the right side of God. I'm a big man, as you see, I could crush a slip of a lad such as you to death, I mean the death that is love, the death I understand love to be. But meet it is that I keep those desires shackled in handcuffs and leg-irons. I'm good at that sort of thing because I'm a policeman by trade. And I'm highly respected. I'm highly respected both in the force and in church. The only place

where I'm not highly respected is in this house. They don't give
a shit for me here. Although I've always been a close relation.
Of a sort. I'm a fine tenor but they never invite me to sing.
I might as well be living in the middle of the Sahara desert.
There are too many women here, that's the trouble. And it's
no use talking to Baldy. He's well away. He lives in another
area, best known to himself. I like health and strength and
intelligent conversation. That's why I took a fancy to you,
chum, apart from the fact that I fancy you. I've got no-one to
talk to. These women treat me like a leper. Even though I am
a relation. Of a sort.

What relation?

Is Lady Withers Jane's mother or sister?

If either is the case why isn't Jane called Lady Jane Withers?
Or perhaps she is. Or perhaps neither is the case? Or perhaps
Mrs Withers is actually the Honorable Mrs Withers? But if
that is the case what does that make Mr Withers? And which
Withers is he anyway? I mean what relation is he to the rest of
the Witherses? And who is Riley?

But if you find me bewildered, anxious, confused, uncertain
and afraid, you also find me content. My life possesses shape.
The house has a very warm atmosphere, as you have no doubt
gleaned. And as you have no doubt noted from my account
I talk freely to all its inhabitants, with the exception of Mr
Withers, to whom no-one talks, to whom no-one refers, with
evidently good reason. But I rarely leave the house. No-one
seems to leave the house. Riley leaves the house but rarely.
He must be a secret policeman. Jane continues to do a great
deal of homework while not apparently attending any school.

Lady Withers never leaves the house. She has guests. She receives guests. Those are the steps I hear on the stairs at night.

VOICE 3

I know your mother has written to you to tell you that I am dead. I am not dead. I am very far from being dead, although lots of people have wished me dead, from time immemorial, you especially. It is you who have prayed for my death, from time immemorial. I have heard your prayers. They ring in my ears. Prayers yearning for my death. But I am not dead.

Well, that is not entirely true, not entirely the case. I'm lying. I'm leading you up the garden path, I'm playing about, I'm having my bit of fun, that's what. Because I am dead. As dead as a doornail. I'm writing to you from my grave. A quick word for old time's sake. Just to keep in touch. An old hullo out of the dark. A last kiss from Dad.

I'll probably call it a day after this canter. Not much more to say. All a bit of a sweat. Why am I taking the trouble? Because of you, I suppose, because you were such a loving son. I'm smiling, as I lie in this glassy grave.

Do you know why I use the word glassy? Because I can see out of it.

Lots of love, son. Keep up the good work.

There's only one thing bothers me, to be quite frank. While there is, generally, absolute silence everywhere, absolute silence throughout all the hours, I still hear, occasionally, a dog barking. I hear this dog. Oh, it frightens me.

VOICE I

They have decided on a name for me. They call me Bobo.
Good morning, Bobo, they say, or, See you in the morning,
Bobo, or, Don't drop a goolie, Bobo, or, Don't forget the
diver, Bobo, or, Keep your eye on the ball, Bobo, or, Keep
this side of the tramlines, Bobo, or, How's the lead in your
pencil, Bobo, or, How's tricks in the sticks, Bobo, or, Don't
get too much gum in your gumboots, Bobo.

The only person who does not call me Bobo is the old man. He
calls me nothing. I call him nothing. I don't see him. He keeps
to his room. I don't go near it. He is old and will die soon.

VOICE 2

The police are looking for you. You may remember that you
are still under twenty-one. They have issued your precise
description to all the organs. They will not rest, they assure
me, until you are found. I have stated my belief that you are
in the hands of underworld figures who are using you as a male
prostitute. I have declared in my affidavit that you have never
possessed any strength of character whatsoever and that you
are palpably susceptible to even the most blatant form of
flattery and blandishment. Women were your downfall, even
as a nipper. I haven't forgotten Françoise the French maid or
the woman who masqueraded under the title of governess, the
infamous Miss Carmichael. You will be found, my boy, and
no mercy will be shown to you.

VOICE I

I'm coming back to you, mother, to hold you in my arms.

I am coming home.

I am coming also to clasp my father's shoulder. Where is the old boy? I'm longing to have a word with him. Where is he? I've looked in all the usual places, including the old summer-house, but I can't find him. Don't tell me he's left home at his age? That would be inexpressibly skittish a gesture, on his part. What have you done with him, mother?

VOICE 2

I'll tell you what, my darling. I've given you up as a very bad job. Tell me one last thing. Do you think the word love means anything?

VOICE 1

I am on my way back to you. I am about to make the journey back to you. What will you say to me?

VOICE 3

I have so much to say to you. But I am quite dead. What I have to say to you will never be said.

elected Grove Press Theater Paperbacks

61-X ARDEN, JOHN / Plays: One (Serjeant Musgrave's Dance; The Workhouse Donkey; Armstrong's Last Goodnight) / $4.95

33-0 AYCKBOURN, ALAN / Absurd Person Singular, Absent Friends, Bedroom Farce: Three Plays / $6.95

08-6 BECKETT, SAMUEL / Endgame / $3.95

33-7 BECKETT, SAMUEL / Happy Days / $4.95

61-5 BECKETT, SAMUEL / Ohio Impromptu, Catastrophe, and What Where: Three Plays / $4.95

04-3 BECKETT, SAMUEL / Waiting for Godot / $4.95

34-8 BRECHT, BERTOLT / Galileo / $4.95

72-0 BRECHT, BERTOLT / The Threepenny Opera / $3.95

11-9 CLURMAN, HAROLD / Nine Plays of the Modern Theater (Waiting for Godot by Samuel Beckett; The Visit by Friedrich Durrenmatt; Tango by Slawomir Mrozek; The Caucasian Chalk Circle by Bertolt Brecht; The Balcony by Jean Genet; Rhinoceros by Eugene Ionesco; American Buffalo by David Mamet; The Birthday Party by Harold Pinter; and Rosencrantz and Guildenstern Are Dead by Tom Stoppard) / $15.95

35-2 COWARD, NOEL / Three Plays (Private Lives; Hay Fever; Blithe Spirit) / $7.95

89-6 DURRENMATT, FRIEDRICH / The Visit / $5.95

44-0 GENET, JEAN / The Balcony / $7.95

90-2 GENET, JEAN / The Maids and Deathwatch: Two Plays / $8.95

22-9 HAYMAN, RONALD / How to Read a Play / $6.95

75-X INGE, WILLIAM / Four Plays (Come Back, Little Sheba; Picnic; Bus Stop; The Dark at the Top of the Stairs) / $8.95

99-9 IONESCO, EUGENE / Exit the King, The Killer and Macbett / $9.95

09-4 IONESCO, EUGENE / Four Plays (The Bald Soprano; The Lesson; The Chairs; Jack or The Submission) $6.95

26 4 IONESCO, EUGENE / Rhinoceros and Other Plays (The Leader; The Future Is in Eggs; or It Takes All Sorts to Make a World) / $6.95

35-2 JARRY, ALFRED / The Ubu Plays (Ubu Rex; Ubu Cuckolded; Ubu Enchained) / $9.95

44-4 KAUFMAN, GEORGE and HART, MOSS / Three Plays (Once in a Lifetime; You Can't Take It With You; The Man Who Came to Dinner) / $8.95

6-4 MAMET, DAVID / American Buffalo / $5.95

49-6 MAMET, DAVID / Glengarry Glen Ross / $6.95

17040-7   MAMET, DAVID / A Life in the Theatre / $9.95
17043-1   MAMET, DAVID / Sexual Perversity in Chicago and The Duck Variations / $7.95
17264-7   MROZEK, SLAWOMIR / Tango / $3.95
17092-X   ODETS, CLIFFORD / Six Plays (Waiting for Lefty; Awake and Sing; Golden Boy; Rocket to the Moon; Till the Day I Die; Paradise Lost) / $7.95
17001-6   ORTON, JOE / The Complete Plays (The Ruffian on the Stair; The Good and Faithful Servant; The Erpingham Camp; Funeral Games; Loot; What the Butler Saw; Entertaining Mr. Sloan) / $9.95
17084-9   PINTER, HAROLD / Betrayal / $6.95
17019-9   PINTER, HAROLD / Complete Works: One (The Birthday Party; The Room; The Dumb Waiter; A Slight Ache; A Night Out; The Black and White; The Examination) $8.95
17020-2   PINTER, HAROLD / Complete Works: Two (The Caretaker; Night School; The Dwarfs; The Collection; The Lover; Five Revue Sketches) / $6.95
17051-2   PINTER, HAROLD / Complete Works: Three (The Homecoming; Landscape; Silence; The Basement; Six Revue Sketches; Tea party [play]; Tea Party [short story]; Mac) / $6.95
17950-1   PINTER, HAROLD / Complete Works: Four (Old Times; No Man's Land; Betrayal; Monologue; Family Voices) / $5.95
17251-5   PINTER, HAROLD / The Homecoming / $5.95
17885-8   PINTER, HAROLD / No Man's Land / $7.95
17539-5   POMERANCE, BERNARD / The Elephant Man / $5.95
17743-6   RATTIGAN, TERENCE / Plays: One (French Without Tears; The Winslow Boy; Harlequinade; The Browning Version) / $5.95
62040-2   SETO, JUDITH ROBERTS / The Young Actor's Workbook / $8.95
17948-X   SHAWN, WALLACE and GREGORY, ANDRÉ / My Dinner with Andre / $6.95
13033-X   STOPPARD, TOM / Rosencrantz and Guildenstern Are Dead / $4.95
17884-X   STOPPARD, TOM / Travesties / $4.95
17206-X   WALEY, ARTHUR, tr. and ed. / The Nō Plays of Japan / $7.95

Available from your local bookstore, or directly from Grove Press. (Add $1.00 postage and handling for the first book and 50¢ for each additional book.)

GROVE PRESS, INC., 920 Broadway, New York, N.Y. 10010

elected Grove Press Paperbacks

4-7   ACKER, KATHY / Blood and Guts in High School / $7.95

0-7   ACKER, KATHY / Great Expectations: A Novel / $6.95

2-1   ALIFANO, ROBERTO / Twenty-four Conversations with Borges, 1980-1983 / $8.95

8-5   ALLEN, DONALD & BUTTERICK, GEORGE F., eds. / The Postmoderns: The New American Poetry Revised 1945-1960 / $12.95

1-7   ALLEN, DONALD M., & TALLMAN, WARREN, eds. / Poetics of the New American Poetry / $14.95

1-X   ARDEN, JOHN / Arden: Plays One (Sergeant Musgrave's Dance, The Workhouse Donkey, Armstrong's Last Goodnight) / $4.95

7-X   ARSAN, EMMANUELLE / Emmanuelle / $3.95

3-2   ARTAUD, ANTONIN / The Theater and Its Double / $7.95

3-5   BARASH, D. and LIPTON, J. / Stop Nuclear War! A Handbook / $7.95

6-9   BARRY, TOM, WOOD, BETH & PREUSCH, DEB / The Other Side of Paradise: Foreign Control in the Caribbean / $11.95

7-3   BARNES, JOHN / Evita—First Lady: A Biography of Eva Peron / $5.95

8-5   BECKETT, SAMUEL / Company / $3.95

9-0   BECKETT, SAMUEL / Disjecta: Miscellaneous Writings and a Dramatic Fragment, ed. Cohn, Ruby / $5.95

8-6   BECKETT, SAMUEL / Endgame / $3.95

3-6   BECKETT, SAMUEL / Ill Seen Ill Said / $4.95

1-5   BECKETT, SAMUEL / Ohio Impromptu, Catastrophe, and What Where: Three Plays / $4.95

4-2   BECKETT, SAMUEL / Rockababy and Other Short Pieces / $3.95

9-X   BECKETT, SAMUEL / Three Novels: Molloy, Malone Dies and The Unnamable / $7.95

4-8   BECKETT, SAMUEL / Waiting for Godot / $4.95

8-1   BERLIN, NORMAND / Eugene O'Neill / $9.95

7-X   BIELY, ANDREW / St. Petersburg / $12.50

2-3   BIRCH, CYRIL & KEENE, DONALD, eds. / Anthology of Chinese Literature, Vol. I: From Early Times to the 14th Century / $17.50

6-5   BIRCH, CYRIL, ed. / Anthology of Chinese Literature, Vol. II: From the 14th Century to the Present / $12.95

4-2   BLOCH, DOROTHY / "So the Witch Won't Eat Me," Fantasy and the Child's Fear of Infanticide / $7.95

0-5   BORGES, JORGE LUIS / Ficciones / $6.95

0-1   BORGES, JORGE LUIS / A Personal Anthology / $6.95

62372-X	BRECHT, BERTOLT / The Caucasian Chalk Circle / $5.95
17109-8	BRECHT, BERTOLT / The Good Woman of Setzuan / $4.50
17112-8	BRECHT, BERTOLT / Galileo / $4.95
17065-2	BRECHT, BERTOLT / The Mother / $7.95
17106-3	BRECHT, BERTOLT / Mother Courage and Her Children / $3.9
17472-0	BRECHT, BERTOLT / Threepenny Opera / $3.95
17393-7	BRETON ANDRE / Nadja / $6.95
13011-9	BULGAKOV, MIKHAIL / The Master and Margarita / $6.95
17108-X	BURROUGHS, WILLIAM S. / Naked Lunch / $4.95
17749-5	BURROUGHS, WILLIAM S. / The Soft Machine, Nova Express, The Wild Boys: Three Novels / $5.95
62488-2	CLARK, AL, ed. / The Film Year Book 1984 / $12.95
17038-5	CLEARY, THOMAS / The Original Face: An Anthology of Rinza Zen / $4.95
17735-5	CLEVE, JOHN / The Crusader Books I and II / $5.95
17411-9	CLURMAN, HAROLD (Ed.) / Nine Plays of the Modern Theater (Waiting for Godot by Samuel Beckett, The Visit by Friedrich Durrenmatt, Tango by Slawomir Mrozek, The Caucasian Chalk Circle by Bertolt Brecht, The Balcony by Jean Genet, Rhinocer by Eugene Ionesco, American Buffalo by David Mamet, The Birthday Party by Harold Pinter, Rosencrantz and Guildenstern Are Dead by Tom Stoppard) / $15.95
17962-5	COHN, RUBY / New American Dramatists: 1960-1980 / $7.95
17971-4	COOVER, ROBERT / Spanking the Maid / $4.95
17535-1	COWARD, NOEL / Three Plays by Noel Coward (Private Lives, Hay Fever, Blithe Spirit) / $7.95
17740-1	CRAFTS, KATHY & HAUTHER, BRENDA / How To Beat the System: The Student's Guide to Good Grades / $3.95
17219-1	CUMMINGS, E.E. / 100 Selected Poems / $5.50
17329-5	DOOLITTLE, HILDA / Selected Poems of H.D. / $9.95
17863-7	DOSS, MARGOT PATTERSON / San Francisco at Your Feet (Second Revised Edition) / $8.95
17398-8	DOYLE, RODGER, & REDDING, JAMES / The Complete Food Handbook (revised any updated edition) / $3.50
17987-0	DURAS, MARGUERITE / Four Novels: The Afternoon of Mr. Andesmas; 10:30 on a Summer Night; Moderato Cantabile; The Square) / $9.95
17246-9	DURRENMATT, FRIEDRICH / The Physicists / $6.95
17239-6	DURRENMATT, FRIEDRICH / The Visit / $5.95
17990-0	FANON, FRANZ / Black Skin, White Masks / $8.95
17327-9	FANON, FRANZ / The Wretched of the Earth / $6.95
17754-1	FAWCETT, ANTHONY / John Lennon: One Day At A Time, A Personal Biography (Revised Edition) / $8.95
17902-1	FEUERSTEIN, GEORG / The Essence of Yoga / $3.95

5-6 FRIED, GETTLEMAN, LEVENSON & PECKENHAM, eds. / Guatemala in Rebellion: Unfinished History / $8.95

3-6 FROMM, ERICH / The Forgotten Language / $8.95

3-9 GARWOOD, DARRELL / Under Cover: Thirty-five Years of CIA Deception / $3.95

2-1 GELBER, JACK / The Connection / $3.95

0-2 GENET, JEAN / The Maids and Deathwatch: Two Plays / $8.95

0-4 GENET, JEAN / The Miracle of the Rose / $7.95

3-5 GENET, JEAN / Our Lady of the Flowers / $8.95

5-2 GETTLEMAN, LACEFIELD, MENASHE, MERMELSTEIN, & RADOSH, eds. / El Salvador: Central America in the New Cold War / $12.95

4-3 GIBBS, LOIS MARIE / Love Canal: My Story / $6.95

8-0 GIRODIAS, MAURICE, ed. / The Olympia Reader / $5.95

7-9 GOMBROWICZ, WITOLD / Three Novels: Ferdydurke, Pornografia and Cosmos / $12.50

4-9 GOVER, ROBERT / One Hundred Dollar Misunderstanding / $2.95

2-7 GREENE, GERALD and CAROLINE / SM: The Last Taboo / $2.95

0-4 GUITAR PLAYER MAGAZINE / The Guitar Player Book (Revised and Updated Edition) $11.95

4-1 HARRIS, FRANK / My Life and Loves / $9.95

6-6 HARWOOD, RONALD / The Dresser / $5.95

3-7 HAVEL, VACLAV, The Memorandum / $5.95

2-9 HAYMAN, RONALD / How To Read A Play / $6.95

5-X HOCHHUTH, ROLF / The Deputy / $7.95

5-8 HOLMES, BURTON / The Olympian Games in Athens: The First Modern Olympics, 1896 / $6.95

1-8 HUMPHREY, DORIS / The Art of Making Dances / $9.95

5-X INGE, WILLIAM / Four Plays (Come Back, Little Sheba; Picnic; Bus Stop; The Dark at the Top of the Stairs) / $8.95

9-9 IONESCO, EUGENE / Exit the King, The Killer, Macbeth / $9.95

9-4 IONESCO, EUGENE / Four Plays (The Bald Soprano, The Lesson, The Chairs, and Jack or The Submission) / $6.95

6-4 IONESCO, EUGENE / Rhinoceros and Other Plays / $6.95

5-2 JARRY, ALFRED / The Ubu Plays (Ubu Rex, Ubu Cuckolded, Ubu Enchained) / $9.95

3-9 JOHNSON, CHARLES / Oxherding Tale / $6.95

4-7 JORGENSEN, ELIZABETH WATIKINS & HENRY IRVIN / Eric Berne, Master Gamesman: A Transactional Biography / $9.95

0-0 KEENE, DONALD, ed. / Japanese Literature: An Introduction for Western Readers-$2.25

1-3 KEENE, DONALD, ed. / Anthology of Japanese Literature: Earliest Era to Mid-19th Century / $13.95

17278-7 KEROUAC, JACK / Dr. Sax / $5.95
17171-3 KEROUAC, JACK / Lonesome Traveler / $5.95
17287-6 KEROUAC, JACK / Mexico City Blues / $9.95
62173-5 KEROUAC, JACK / Satori in Paris / $4.95
17035-0 KERR, CARMEN / Sex for Women Who Want to Have Fun and
        Loving Relationships With Equals / $9.95
17981-1 KINGSLEY, PHILIP / The Complete Hair Book: The Ultimate
        Guide to Your Hair's Health and Beauty / $10.95
62424-6 LAWRENCE, D.H. / Lady Chatterley's Lover / $3.95
17178-0 LESTER, JULIUS / Black Folktales / $5.95
17481-X LEWIS, MATTHEW / The Monk / $12.50
17391-0 LINSSEN, ROBERT / Living Zen / $12.50
17114-4 MALCOLM X (Breitman., ed.) / Malcolm X Speaks / $6.95
17023-7 MALRAUX, ANDRE/The Conquerors/$3.95
17068-7 MALRAUX, ANDRE/Lazarus/$2.95
17093-8 MALRAUX, ANDRE / Man's Hope / $12.50
17016-4 MAMET, DAVID / American Buffalo / $5.95
62049-6 MAMET, DAVID / Glengarry Glenn Ross / $6.95
17040-7 MAMET, DAVID / A Life in the Theatre / $9.95
17043-1 MAMET, DAVID / Sexual Perversity in Chicago & The Duck
        Variations / $7.95
17471-2 MILLER, HENRY / Black Spring / $4.95
62375-4 MILLER, HENRY / Tropic of Cancer / $7.95
62379-7 MILLER, HENRY / Tropic of Capricorn / $7.95
17933-1 MROZEK, SLAWOMIR / Three Plays: Striptease, Tango,
        Vatzlav / $12.50
13035-6 NERUDA, PABLO / Five Decades: Poems 1925-1970.
        bilingual ed. / $14.50
62243-X NICOSIA, GERALD / Memory Babe: A Critical Biography of Jack
        Kerouac / $11.95
17092-X ODETS, CLIFFORD / Six Plays (Waiting for Lefty, Awake and
        Sing, Golden Boy, Rocket to the Moon, Till the Day I Die,
        Paradise Lost) / $7.95
17650-2 OE, KENZABURO / A Personal Matter / $6.95
17002-4 OE, KENZABURO / Teach Us To Outgrow Our Madness (The
        Day He Himself Shall Wipe My Tears Away; Prize Stock; Teach
        Us to Outgrow Our Madness; Aghwee The Sky Monster) / $4.9
17992-7 PAZ, OCTAVIO / The Labyrinth of Solitude / $10.95
17084-9 PINTER, HAROLD / Betrayal / $6.95
17232-9 PINTER, HAROLD / The Birthday Party & The Room / $6.95
17251-5 PINTER, HAROLD / The Homecoming / $5.95
17539-5 POMERANCE / The Elephant Man / $5.95
62013-9 PORTWOOD, DORIS / Common Sense Suicide: The Final
        Right / $8.00

3-8 REAGE, PAULINE / The Story of O, Part II; Return to the Chateau / $3.95

9-7 RECHY, JOHN / City of Night / $4.50

1-9 RECHY, JOHN / Numbers / $8.95

7-8 ROBBE-GRILLET, ALAIN / (Djinn and La Maison de Rendez-Vous) / $8.95

3-8 ROBBE—GRILLET, ALAIN / For a New Novel: Essays on Fiction / $9.95

7-9 ROBBE-GRILLET, ALAIN / The Voyeur / 6.95

0-9 ROSSET, BARNEY, ed. / Evergreen Review Reader: 1962-1967 / $12.50

3-X ROSSET, PETER and VANDERMEER, JOHN / The Nicaragua Reader: Documents of a Revolution under Fire / $9.95

6-1 RULFO, JUAN / Pedro Paramo / $3.95

2-7 SADE, MARQUIS DE / Justine; Philosophy in the Bedroom; Eugenie de Franval; and Other Writings / $14.95

9-X SANTINI, ROSEMARIE / The Secret Fire: How Women Live Their Sexual Fantasies / $3.95

5-5 SCHEFFLER, LINDA / Help Thy Neighbor: How Counseling Works and When It Doesn't / $7.95

3-6 SCHNEEBAUM, TOBIAS / Keep the River on Your Right / $12.50

2-4 SELBY, HUBERT, JR. / Last Exit to Brooklyn / $8.95

3-X SHAWN, WALLACE, & GREGORY, ANDRE / My Dinner with Andre / $6.95

6-3 SIEGAL AND SIEGAL / AIDS: The Medical Mystery / $7.95

7-4 SINGH, KHUSHWANT / Train to Pakistan / $4.50

7-5 SNOW, EDGAR / Red Star Over China / $11.95

9-0 SRI NISARGADATA MAHARAJ / Seeds of Consciousness / $9.95

3-4 STEINER, CLAUDE / Healing Alcoholism / $7.95

6-9 STEINER, CLAUDE / The Other Side of Power / $8.95

6-1 STOPPARD, TOM / Jumpers / $6.95

3-X STOPPARD, TOM / Rosencrantz and Guildenstern Are Dead / $4.95

4-X STOPPARD, TOM / Travesties / $4.95

9-4 STRYK, LUCIEN, ed. / The Crane's Bill: Zen Poems of China and Japan / $5.95

0-2 SUZUKI, D.T. / Introduction to Zen Buddhism / $11.95

4-8 SUZUKI, D.T. / Manual of Zen Buddhism / $9.95

9-9 THELWELL, MICHAEL / The Harder They Come: A Novel about Jamaica / $7.95

0-8 TOOLE, JOHN KENNEDY / A Confederacy of Dunces / $6.95

3-8 TROCCHI, ALEXANDER / Cain's Book / $3.50

3-9 TUTUOLA, AMOS / The Palm-Wine Drunkard / $4.50

9-1 UNGERER, TOMI / Far Out Isn't Far Enough (Illus.) / $12.95

0-3 VITHOULKAS, GEORGE / The Science of Homeopathy / $12.50

13021-6	WALEY, ARTHUR / The Book of Songs / $8.95
17211-6	WALEY, ARTHUR / Monkey / $8.95
17207-8	WALEY, ARTHUR / The Way and Its Power: A Study of the T
	Te Ching and Its Place in Chinese Thought / $9.95
17418-6	WATTS, ALAN W. / The Spirit of Zen / $6.95
62031-3	WORTH, KATHERINE / Oscar Wilde / $8.95
17739-8	WYCKOFF, HOGIE / Solving Problems Together / $7.95

GROVE PRESS, INC., 920 Broadway, New York, N.Y. 10010

If you would like to receive, free of charge, regular information about new plays and theatre books from Methuen, please send your name and address to:

The Marketing Department (Drama)
Methuen London Ltd
North Way
Andover
Hampshire SP10 5BE